Industry,
Prices and
Markets

Industry, Prices and Markets

W DUNCAN REEKIE

University of Edinburgh

A HALSTED PRESS BOOK

John Wiley & Sons
New York

First published 1979 by

PHILIP ALLAN PUBLISHERS LIMITED
MARKET PLACE
DEDDINGTON
OXFORD OX5 4SE

PUBLISHED IN THE USA
BY HALSTED PRESS, A DIVISION
OF JOHN WILEY & SONS, INC.,
NEW YORK.

Library of Congress Cataloging in Publication Data

Reekie, W Duncan.
    Industry, prices, and markets.

    'A Halsted Press book.'
    1. Industrial organization (Economic theory)
2. Competition. 3. Austrian school of economists.
I. Title
HD2326.R43   338.6   79—14543
ISBN 0—470—26709—7

Set by MHL Typesetting Ltd, Coventry
Printed in Great Britain at
The Camelot Press Ltd, Southampton

For Ruth, Basil and Natalie

Contents

Preface

This text is an addition to the already crowded field of industrial organisation. Books on the subject abound on both sides of the Atlantic. Most of these contain large sections on price theory, the theory of the firm, reviews of empirical studies and details of the legal framework affecting both the structure and conduct of industry. No textbook, however, has yet tackled the topic in the way attempted here.

This is the only claim I can make for novelty. The book is intended for those who have had some previous exposure to elementary economics, and is simply a text, not a contribution to knowledge. The need for a novel synthesis at this level of existing, more advanced material, is highlighted in several ways. First, the conventional structure/conduct/ performance model has had serious doubts cast on its validity by the empirical studies of economists such as Bodoff, Brozen and Demsetz. These studies have mostly been carried out in the 1970s and so as yet have had little opportunity to appear in the textbook literature.

Second, the received theories of price and of the firm are under attack from a diversity of directions. Writers with approaches as different as Baumol, Dewey, Loasby, Marris, Joan Robinson and Williamson join together in a common concern over the inadequacy of much of contemporary theory as an instrument for aiding prediction and policy formulation. Despite this anxiety one particular school of thought has received little attention in the textbook literature. This is the Austrian approach developed by Mises and Hayek, and most recently by Kirzener.

I attempt to remedy this omission here. The Austrian view that profits arise from *ex ante* entrepreneurial activity rather than from an *ex post* monopoly market structure is more in line with the results of the empirical studies referred to above than is the structure/conduct/performance paradigm of neo-classical price theory.

Third, although Coase, as long ago as 1937, attempted to apply economic analysis *within* the firm as well as *between* firms *within* the market, it was not until the 1970s that Alchian and Demsetz, and later Williamson, developed theories which seem (to me at least) to offer more promise for further development than did Coase's original and now classic treatment. I attempt to synthesise their contribution with that of the general Austrian approach.

There are thus three major gaps in the textbook literature on industrial organisation. Two of these, one empirical and one theoretical derive from material new to the profession. The other, which is theoretical, has been long neglected but explains the facts more satisfactorily than does conventional theory.

This book attempts to fill these gaps. To provide a foundation, some standard analyses and data are also provided. Still more are omitted. Thus the book should be read in conjunction with either lecture material or with a text of a more conventional nature. For example, most of the topics covered in a normal price theory course, plus the newer theories of the firm, and the British legal framework relating to monopolies and restrictive practices, are dealt with in my *Managerial Economics* (Philip Allan, 1975). Their repetition here would impose a needless cost on author and reader alike.

W. DUNCAN REEKIE
Fordell, 1978

Industrial organisation is a field that is in deep intellectual trouble. The source of that trouble is that old textbook theory that we all know so well.

Richard R. Nelson
Bell Journal of Economics, 1976.

1

Introduction

This quote summarises why this book was written. There is reason to be acutely dissatisfied with the state of economics as it relates to industry. The disquiet does *not* stem from the fact that the 'theory is not realistic'; this is not necessarily a valid reason for dissatisfaction. Theory, by definition, must be abstract and general and cannot describe the minutiae of each case.

Discontent is due rather to the fact that industrial organisation is a field of intellectual muddle. Industrial economists contradict each other, they commence their analyses from opposing premises, and they pursue unrelated theories. This is particularly discomfiting given the centrality of the topic of industrial organisation to the study of economics. Economists want to know why and how indefinite but limited resources are transformed into specific goods and services for final consumption. It is industry (and the firms that make up industry) which carries out this transformation. If a study of industry is fundamental to a study of economics as a whole, then industrial economics as a subject should have a theoretical framework which, if not flawless, should be internally consistent and provide pointers as to the direction in which both future theoreticians and policy makers should move.

The remaining pages of this chapter outline the main

reasons for the present discontent with industrial economics and provide an indication of how the subject could develop. It will be asserted that the subject has been dominated either by the British (or engineering) approach or the American (or industry structure) approach. An alternative approach, which we will suggest is more fruitful, derives from a long-neglected tradition, sometimes known as 'Austrian economics'. This stresses the importance of the entrepreneur and the competitive process. The Austrian view, it will be found, is much more successful in explaining real life industrial behaviour than the British or American traditions. If one theory explains or predicts events better than another then that theory merits serious consideration. On this ground alone, the Austrian approach has not received due attention by economists. It will be argued, moreover, that not only does a study of the entrepreneur and the competitive process explain industrial behaviour in a satisfactory manner, it also helps provide better normative evaluations of the workings of the industrial economy.

We will now outline these three schools of thought in some more detail. The engineering tradition fails to explain some apparent paradoxes such as the continued coexistence of large and small firms. It also fails to explain why firms should exist at all. The structuralist approach assumes that information is universally and costlessly available. It even precludes rivalry between entrepreneurs. This can result in the textbook model of perfect competition being regarded as some kind of ideal and so may result in misleading policy inferences. The Austrian approach, however, studies the competitive process itself and examines how information is acquired and disseminated. It focuses on the role of the entrepreneur and also on the firm of whatever size as the agent or agents which bring together buyers and sellers into situations of mutually beneficial exchange.

(a) IS INDUSTRIAL ORGANISATION AN ENGINEERING PROBLEM?

Is industrial organisation a problem for the engineer?

In the 1930s through to the 1960s the answer was an implicit but emphatic 'Yes'. The two leading British texts were Professor Sir Austin Robinson's *The Structure of Competitive Industry*[1] and Professor P. Sargant Florence's *The Logic of British and American Industry*.[2] Robinson emphasised the concept of the optimum size of firm. He analysed the five criteria of technique, management, finance, marketing and risk. Each of these could have different optimum scales of operation and the reconciliation of these optima was essentially an exercise in organisational logic.

Florence, even in his 1972 edition, provided a distinction between 'economy' and 'efficiency' which can only be described as semantic and which reinforces the view that the optimal organisation of industry is merely a more or less complicated engineering problem. 'Efficiency takes cost as given and focuses attention upon return . . . economy or elimination of waste takes return . . . as given and focuses attention upon the cost incurred. To be economical . . . implies that . . . cost is lowered. The standpoint of both efficiency and economy may be combined by defining a *logical organisation of industry* as one that as far as possible *yields maximum return or product at minimum cost*'. (p. 59, emphasis in original.)

Florence then goes on to develop his theme that large-scale organisation is logical when there are increasing returns to scale due to the three principles: bulk transactions, massed reserves and multiples. Small-scale organisations will, however, continue to flourish in those fields where demand is limited, or where transportation costs to or from a large-scale centralised plant outweigh the higher production costs involved in manufacturing in a variety of locations on a restricted scale but close to the sources of raw materials or to customers.

All this seemed at first sight to be eminently sensible. Both Robinson and Florence referred back to Adam Smith and the principle of division of labour. Yet their conclusions could have been deduced just as readily by an industrial engineer. How did their 'logic' differ from the approach of

Smith? Did it differ? Adam Smith's original view is that 'division of labour, from which so many advantages are derived, is not originally the effect of any human wisdom, which foresees and intends that general opulence to which it gives occasion. It is the necessary, though very slow and gradual consequence of a certain propensity in human nature which has in view no such exclusive utility; the propensity to truck, barter and exchange one thing for another'.[3] Thus division of labour according to Smith is the result of a market process. It is the result of trade and exchange. Trade and exchange determine (through the linkage of division of labour) industrial organisation. The task of economists, then, is not to examine the engineering linkages between division of labour and industries and firms. That can be left to the engineer within whose area of competence the problem lies. The task of the economist is to ascertain how mutually beneficial trades result in certain forms of industrial organisation and, conversely, what forms of industrial organisation maximise the benefits of trading between willing buyers and sellers.

This task is rarely tackled in the literature on industrial economics: it should be. Economists should leave engineering to the engineers and return to their lasts.

(b) WHY IS PERFECT COMPETITION 'PERFECT'?

A second reason for discontent with the current state of industrial economics is the use of the adjective 'perfect'. In 1962 Professor T. Wilson[4] wrote: ' "Perfect Competition" is not a norm and the fact that it has been taken for one is a remarkable example of the way in which we can mislead ourselves with our own emotive terminology. Indeed the expression "perfect competition" has probably done more to darken counsel than any other in modern economic literature . . . '

We are rightly warned against attributing values to the word 'perfect'. Why? One obvious reason is that 'perfect' competition may not be possible in an industry composed of firms of 'optimal' scale. The diffuse market structure of perfect competition is not compatible with the small numbers of firms which exist in industries where scale economies are not exhausted until each firm has secured a large and significant share of the market at any given price.

Another reason for unease with 'perfect competition' is that it is the concept which underpins the 'structure/conduct/performance' model of industrial economics. While students in Britain studied Florence and Robinson, their contemporaries in America were being influenced by the work of writers such as Professor Joe S. Bain. In his book *Industrial Organisation* Bain sees a direct causal link between structure and performance.[5] Implicitly and explicitly a perfectly competitive market structure is more desirable than a more concentrated one. As a consequence he recommends (pp. 504–5) that 'control of market structures should be a major tool of policy in remedying or averting monopolistic price or profit tendencies ... (1) by requiring dissolution ... of existing dominant firms into several parts ... (2) by reducing entry barriers ... (3) by ... induc(ing) lesser degrees of product differentiation ... the policy could go further and attack ... very high seller concentration ... as a *precautionary measure*' (emphasis in original).

Disquiet should not be occasioned by the drastic nature of Bain's proposals. Rather we should be perturbed that they are based on a diagnosis which employs the analytic methods of the structure/conduct/performance paradigm. Bain himself was the first to explicitly delineate this model in earlier pages of his book (pp. 7–12). But the alleged importance of market structure as a predictor of business conduct, and so performance, flows directly from a dominance of an engineering rather than a market approach to economics. The approach inevitably results in 'perfect' competition being regarded as an ideal. Lord Robbins is widely quoted as saying that economics 'is the science which studies human behaviour as a relationship between ends and means which have alternative uses'.[6] This is at once misleading, incomplete and imprecise. Where ends and means are given (as is implicit in this definition), resource allocation *per se* is a problem which can be solved by pure mathematical logic. All that is required is that the marginal rates of substitution between any two commodities or factors be the same in all their different uses. Study of the competitive process is thus unnecessary and optimal allocation can be obtained either by the achievement of equilibrium in a perfectly competitive market or by the calculations of an omnicompetent mind. The problem is then purely technological, not economic. The misleading nature of the adjective 'perfect' flows directly from this definition of economics. It can be shown, using the assumptions of perfect competition, that welfare is maximised only when price equals marginal cost for all commodities and that this condition only holds in a perfectly competitive equilibrium. It then follows that monopolistic and oligopolistic market structures, and Chamberlinian situations of monopolistic competition, can be deemed inefficient and undesirable.

The economic problem, however, is not how the most efficient allocation of given resources can be achieved in order to best attain known goals. Rather, as Hayek argues, it is concerned with 'how to secure the best use of resources known to any of the members of the society, for ends whose relative importance only these individuals know'.[7] The relevant framework is not one of given ends and given means. It is a matter of generating sufficient information to permit and encourage willing buyers and sellers to maximise the net gains which would accrue to them through the process of exchange.

Economics is concerned with choice in the presence of uncertainty. If we assume (realistically) the absence of an omnicompetent mind and (desirably) the lack of coercion in society, then a study of industrial organisation can help us to understand how the problem is solved. A perfectly competitive market structure in equilibrium is not the answer. What is required is an understanding of why people act, decide, and choose in the way they do in the presence of uncertainty about the consequences of their actions. In a world of uncertainty, changing tastes and evolving technologies *no* structural equilibrium *qua* equilibrium can be optimal. In fact, in such a world the word 'equilibrium' really has no meaning. Attention must be redirected towards conduct and performance, towards the competitive process itself.

(c) THE COMPETITIVE PROCESS AND THE DIVISION OF KNOWLEDGE

How does the competitive process of trade and exchange work? If markets imply the 'propensity to truck, barter and exchange' in the presence of uncertainty and imperfect information, how can efficient use of knowledge (itself a scarce commodity) be ensured?

To the economist each individual has a large store of two types of private knowledge. First there are preferences, particularly consumer preferences. A consumer's preferences are generally unknown to others until he discloses them by choosing one product against another. Similarly, a worker's job preferences are revealed when he pursues a particular occupation. Preferences are private knowledge until actions reveal them.

Second, there is the knowledge of being in a unique situation: the knowledge of the 'man on the spot'. For instance, the manager of an electric showroom and repair shop knows his workers' skills, their personalities, how well they get on with each other, where to hire part-time labour, which equipment is in good condition, which is likely to need repair, where to get spare parts, where to get stock if supplies are interrupted, when business is likely to be busy and when slack, his customers' particular needs, and so on. This is essentially private knowledge since the manager is in a unique location, dealing with unique individuals, servicing and using unique equipment and the like. Clearly, production decisions must somehow take the unique knowledge of this and other such 'men on the spot' into account.

But efficiency requires more than that production decisions be based on private knowledge. There must exist a means by which each producer's decisions tend to coordinate with the decisions of all the other producers and consumers in the market. On the face of it, this appears impossible. How is an individual to coordinate his decisions with those of millions of others when their decisions are at least partly based on private knowledge which he does not possess? Private knowledge of the kind described cannot, by its very nature, be conveyed in the statistical aggregates of central or governmental plans. These require data reduction and foreknowledge, both of which are, by definition, precluded from private knowledge. To fully appreciate these problems, we need to consider how production and consumption decisions are coordinated by the price mechanism.

Hayek explains the operation thus:

> Fundamentally, in a system in which the knowledge of the relevant facts is dispersed among many people, prices can act to coordinate the separate actions of different people. . . . It is worth contemplating for a moment a very simple and commonplace instance of the action of the price system to see what precisely it accomplishes. Assume that somewhere in the world a new opportunity for the use of some raw material, say, tin, has arisen, or that one of the sources of supply of tin has been eliminated. It does not matter for our purpose — and it is significant that it does not matter — which of these two causes has made tin more scarce. All that the users of tin need to know is that some of the tin they used to consume is now more profitably employed elsewhere and that, in consequence, they must economise tin. There is no need for the great majority of them even to know where the more urgent need has arisen, or in favour of what other needs they ought to husband the supply. If only some of them know directly of the new demand, and switch resources over to it, and if the people who are aware of the new gap thus created in turn fill it from still other sources, the effect will rapidly spread throughout the whole economic system and influence not only all the uses of tin but also those of its substitutes and the substitutes of these substitutes, the supply of all things made of tin, and their substitutes, and so on; and all this without the great majority of those instrumental in bringing about these substitutions knowing anything at all about the original cause of these changes. The whole acts as one market, not because any of its members survey the whole field, but because their limited individual fields of vision sufficiently over-

lap so that through many intermediaries the relevant information is communicated to all. The mere fact that there is one price for any commodity — or rather that local prices are connected in a manner determined by the cost of transport, etc. — brings about the solution which (it is just conceptually possible) might have been arrived at by one single mind possessing all the information which is in fact dispersed among all the people involved in the process.[7]

The 'solution' referred to is, of course, perfectly competitive equilibrium. Thus it would seem that we have come full circle and returned to the structure/conduct/performance model. Not so. Hayek would be the first to ask why we are concerned with this 'admittedly fictitious state of equilibrium'? His explicit response, implicit above, is that 'the only justification for this is the supposed existence of a tendency towards equilibrium'.[8] The tendency exists because of the information prices convey to entrepreneurs. Differentials between bid and offer prices signal to entrepreneurs that profits are available if by their actions they can narrow the spread. Entrepreneurship is the essence of the competitive process. It is an equilibrating force, moving bid and offer prices closer together.

Because knowledge is divided among millions of individuals with no one knowing more than a tiny part, factors of production are often employed where they make less than the maximum contribution. A producer may be unaware that a factor could make a greater contribution in another employment. Those who know of other employments may be unaware of the availability of the factor.[9]

To correct such misallocations the price system (1) provides a means of discovering resource misdirection, (2) stimulates use of the means of discovery, (3) encourages transfer of resource control to producers who have discovered such misallocations, and (4) rewards their corrections.

Suppose for example, tin is being used to make products on which consumers place low values, and/or it is being used where each ton of tin contributes little to physical output. In these cases, each ton of tin makes only a small contribution to the revenues of the manufacturer using it.

As a result, manufacturers place low values on tin, and it can be obtained for a low price. Now suppose an entrepreneur surveys the situation and discovers what he believes to be a more profitable way of using tin: by making a product which he hopes consumers will value highly and/or by using a method of production which gets more output per unit input. If he is wrong — and has overestimated the prices consumers will pay and/or underestimated his costs — he will fare no better than most other producers and have little impact on the market. If he is right, however, he will soon earn high profits because each ton of tin will make a large contribution to his revenues. His profits will encourage and enable him to expand and he will bid more tin away from other producers. Other firms will notice his profits, stop using tin in the old and relatively unproductive employments, and start copying his use of tin. This will result in competitive bidding raising the price of tin so reflecting its more productive use. Simultaneously, increased output will reduce the price of the entrepreneur's product. Competition ensures that the entrepreneur has no guarantee of permanent profits.

Of course, anyone can look back and assert which producers were the next most successful in using each factor of production where it made the greatest contribution. But no one can look forward, before the fact, and assert which producer will prove to be the most efficient. That has to be decided by the competitive process itself.

In summary, the competitive process provides incentives and so evokes effort. It generates a continuous and universal search for substitutes, for ways of replacing the less desirable by the more desirable. This process of substitution begins with the consumer seeking to distribute his income to the best advantage and passes on to the producer striving to replace the less by the more sought after goods and substituting a better way of producing for a worse way. The essence of the process is choice by the consumer; emulation, rivalry and substitution by the producer.

By competition we ought to mean mobility, not equilibrium. We ought to mean the unbarred movement of factors of production from low reward occupations to high reward ones: the unbarred movement of consumer patronage from high-priced to low-priced suppliers of identical goods. For this to occur knowledge that such movement is worthwhile is required. This is the function of the entrepreneur: to seek out such opportunities before others perceive them. Rivalry is of the essence in this process. But rivalry, indeed even the very verb 'to compete', is precluded from the equilibrium of 'perfect competition'.[10] Any competitive action by a businessman (for example, a price cut) is regarded in pure theory as evidence that he possesses some monopoly power. Yet what kind of market power is it that a 'non-perfectly competitive' businessman has? The power is no more or less than that of the odd-job man who advertises his services in a small town newspaper. He could charge a higher price or a lower price if he so wishes. But if he also wishes to maximise his income or wealth he is constrained by the market to charge the profit maximising price. Such 'monopoly power' is as relevant as the power each of us has to give away our wealth.

The trial-and-error price cuts or increases made by businessmen are simply examples of ways they attempt to gain information as to where the profit maximising price is. Trial and error price adjustments, advertising decisions, product variations and other forms of rivalry are merely methods of gleaning market information in situations where knowledge is imperfect and costly to obtain.

This exclusion of rivalry, this exclusion of the competitive process, from the definition of perfect competition is but little mentioned in the literature. This is profoundly disturbing. If, as Adam Smith claimed, wealth is created by trade, if buyers and sellers can never fully know of each other's offerings then the received static theory is sterile. Indeed the 'invisible hand' has no place in such a theory. The industrial economist should bring the rivalrous competitive process back to the centre of the economic stage. Only then can industrial organisation, and possibly economics as a whole, cease to be in 'deep intellectual trouble'.

(d) A PREVIEW

Chapter 2 examines briefly how the 'engineering' approach to industrial organisation has resulted in the as yet unresolved paradox that while giant firms and plants are 'logical' the market 'illogically' permits small and medium-sized ones to continue to exist. The implications for policy makers given varied and changing consumer tastes and production possibilities are obviously unclear.

In Chapter 3 the standard neo-classical case for perfectly competitive behaviour is presented. The problems which such a prescription would face are detailed and the ingenious and intelligent theoretical developments which have been made in an attempt to solve these problems are set out. These attempts are shown to have been unsuccessful.

Chapter 4 provides empirical evidence which denies the validity of the structure/conduct/performance model. The evidence is of comparatively recent origin and contradicts most previous data. The fact that it has taken so long to produce the evidence (and the explanations which go with it) countering earlier studies supporting the neo-classical industrial organisation theory helps explain, in turn, why the Austrian approach has suffered such lengthy neglect. Chapter 5 attacks the traditional theory on its own ground and shows how it leads inexorably to viewing competition as a dynamic process, not an equilibrium condition.

Chapter 6 then examines competition and entrepreneurship in detail. The role of the entrepreneur is analytically distinguished from all others in the production and exchange process. Chapter 7 examines the firm, and identifies the role of the entrepreneur *within* the corporate entity. Chapter 8 concludes by detailing what policy implications the overall discussion has for areas as diverse as anti-trust laws, attitudes to advertising, public utility regulation, profits and nationalisation.

REFERENCES

1 E.A.G. Robinson, *The Structure of Competitive Industry*, Cambridge University Press 1931.
2 P. Sargant Florence, *The Logic of British and American Industry*, Routledge and Kegan Paul, 3rd edition, 1972.
3 Adam Smith, *The Wealth of Nations*, (A. Skinner ed.), Penguin 1975, p. 117.
4 T. Wilson, 'Restrictive practices' in J.P. Miller (ed.) *Competition, Cartels and their Regulation*, North Holland 1962, p. 119.
5 J.S. Bain, *Industrial Organisation*, Wiley 1959.
6 L. Robbins, *The Nature and Significance of Economic Science,* Macmillan 1935, p. 16.
7 F.A. Hayek, 'The use of knowledge in society', *American Economic Review* 1945.
8 F.A. Hayek, 'Economics and knowledge', *Economica* 1937.
9 B. Summers, 'The division of knowledge', *The Freeman* 1977.
10 P.J. McNulty, 'Economic theory and the meaning of competition', *Quarterly Journal of Economics* 1968.

*Granting the advantages of mechanical and
human specialisation, large-scale production,
especially when conducted in large-scale
firms and plants, results in maximum efficiency.*

P. Sargant Florence
Logic of Industrial Organisation, 1933

2

'Logic` and Fact

In this chapter we examine the assertions of the engineering
school that long-run average cost curves display substantial
scale economies in most industries. It will be noted that
the debate over whether these curves are L-shaped or U-
shaped centred on the problem of managerial coordination.
Two factors were neglected in that debate. First, and most
obviously, coordination is only required where change (in
either supply or demand conditions) is tending to occur.
The protagonists ignored the fact that a situation of change
is almost, if not totally, universal. The arguments used were
devoid of any meaningful policy implications. Second, the
definition of long-run average cost curves was overlooked.
Even in orthodox textbooks they are referred to as 'plan-
ning curves.' They are *ex ante* subjective concepts in the
minds of entrepreneurs. Implicitly this means they are
extremely difficult, if not impossible, to estimate from
historic data. Explicitly it means they embody a range of
production possibilities (not only of output rate but also
of product type) only some of which may ultimately
eventuate. The width of the range of choice which is
provided by entrepreneurs to consumers is emphasised by
example in the latter pages of this chapter. The uncertainty
that the entrepreneur must bear as he attempts to anticipate consumer tastes and production techniques is obvious.

The consequences of failure to anticipate correctly is that trade and exchange will not occur. In short, sales will not be made and firms will lose market position. In this manner the competitive process operates and firms do not come to dominate industries permanently. Illustrations from British and American industry are used to show how short lived market dominance often is. In this way, the apparent 'illogic' of much industrial organisation can be better understood.

(a) 'THE BIGGER THE BETTER'

Does the quotation from Sargant Florence at the beginning of this chapter imply that long-run average cost curves are not U-shaped? Are decreasing returns to scale non-existent or unimportant? Should industries be encouraged to assume ever more concentrated structures? Would larger and larger firm and plant sizes be desirable?

Sargant Florence's statement does not go all the way to answering 'yes' to these questions. But he did argue in his book that most industries in both Britain and America operated on too small a scale, and that this was 'an illogical organisation'. This fundamental weakness, he submitted, was due to excessive and increasing variety in consumers' demands. The only possible remedies were either official restrictions of competition by licensing or through the ultimate victory of the more efficient large-scale firms.[1]

Kaldor,[2] in 1934, argued that if large-scale firms are not more efficient, if long-run average cost curves do turn up after passing some optimum point, then the presumption must be made that the function of management is in some sense indivisible. For whatever reason, it must be impossible to add increments of managers to increments of other factors for a proportional expansion of output. Kaldor then asserted that it was difficult to see why more routine functions should not be divisible. Therefore any problem must lie with non-routine, dynamic functions, particularly those associated with the need for coordinated response to change. But in perfect static equilibrium there would be no change and hence no need for coordination. Hence, Kaldor concluded, in conditions of equilibrium firms must be subject to either constant or increasing returns to scale.

(b) CONSTRAINTS ON SIZE

In conventional theory, if constant or increasing returns replace a situation where previously all long-run cost curves had been U-shaped, then each industry will be monopolised by its most efficient firm. Casual observation indicates that this has not happened. Why?

Two main groups of reasons have been advanced. One view suggests that while there may be no effective restraints on the size of firms there are certainly constraints on their rates of growth. Growth is costly, and if growth is pursued at too rapid a rate the costs of growth rise disproportionately. The decision makers in the firm will therefore decide not to move from one profit maximising equilibrium to another (superior) one. If they did then after deduction of costs of movement from the original to the new equilibrium the net present value of the wealth arising from the latter would in fact be smaller than the equivalent wealth which would arise from remaining a non-monopolist* (see pages 138–9 in Chapter 7).

The second group of reasons why there are not monopolies in most industries came from the originator of the idea of the optimum firm, Austin Robinson[3] and, some two decades later, from George Stigler.[4] Like Kaldor, both Robinson and Stigler accepted Adam Smith's view that 'division of labour is limited by the extent of the market', but neither found that to be incompatible with the continued existence of non-monopolistic industries.

---

* Variants on this theme include other theories of the firm where the decision makers are alleged to pursue objective functions other than profits, e.g. sales maximisation, managerial utility and growth rate. For a summary see my *Managerial Economics*, Chapter 2, Philip Allan 1975.

Robinson began by accepting that both large and small plants continued to exist side by side. He agreed with Kaldor that the key to the problem lay in the character of the management function and especially in the character of the task of making internally consistent, coordinated responses to exogenous change. This non-routine coordinating capacity could not be increased by, say, increasing the size of the senior management group. Since then everything to be considered would have to pass through the mind of every (additional) member of that (larger) group. By analogy he argued that unit costs of coordination rise with output. But here Robinson disagreed with Kaldor that such changes were incompatible with standard equilibrium theory (p. 250).

> In Mr Kaldor's world there must be neither sun nor rain, neither snow nor frost, neither thunder nor lightning. There must be a steady consumption of raw materials without any exhaustion of their supplies, a steady progress of firms without such progress bringing either experience to the younger or age to the older. Men must not die, and therefore if the state is to be stationary they must not be born. There must be no inventions, no discoveries of new materials or sources of supply. No machinery must wear out, for it would be impossible to coordinate production during the replacement. In Mr Kaldor's long period we shall not only be dead but in Nirvana.

Robinson then went on to suggest that one could without difficulty envisage conditions which were essentially 'stationary' from the point of view of the industry or the economy but where numerous important, non-routine, coordinated decisions were daily required of individual managements. He continued (p. 252):

> The main unit of coordination is the plant, and Mr Kaldor, if I understand him right, would regard the plant as the firm in this case. A multiplication of plants here yields no economies except in so far as the central office organisation creates conditions nearer to those of perfect competition as regards the distribution of orders to plants and the closing down of plants.

Thus he concluded (p. 256):

> An optimum firm with a definite upper limit imposed by the difficulties and costs of coordination is both logically satisfactory and a necessary hypothesis to explain the facts.

So Robinson came remarkably close to rejecting neo-classical equilibrium theory. Coordination he regarded as a crucial factor. But coordination is only required in non-equilibrium situations. Non-stationary situations, however, were restricted in his analysis to the firm and not extended to the industry or the economy. Had he embraced the notion that the whole purpose of transactions in the market place is to coordinate the ever-changing wants of consumers with the ever-changing abilities of producers he would have found himself in the awkward situation of asking why coordination is sometimes undertaken by the market, and only sometimes in the firm?*

(c) COORDINATION IS DIVISIBLE

Stigler,[4] like Robinson, accepted that division of labour is limited by the extent of the market. Like Robinson, he found it paradoxical that all industries should not, therefore, be monopolised. He resolved the paradox in a different way, however. A paraphrase of Robinson's position might read 'division of labour is limited by the extent of the market except for the function of coordination, which is a special case, and which is indivisible and to which there are some kind of decreasing returns resulting in an optimum firm size'. Stigler saw all functions as being divisible, not excluding coordination. The reason some industries are organised differently from others, he argued, is due to the stage of the industry's life cycle.

He put forward the following theory and illustrated it with reference to diagram 2.1. Vertical integration will be extensive in young industries; disintegration will be observed as an industry grows; and reintegration will take place as an industry passes into decline. These life cycle effects are illustrated by reference to a multi-process product, each process having its own distinct cost function. Some of these processes display individually falling cost

* See Chapter 7.

curves, others rise continuously, and still others have U-shaped cost curves.

Why then does the firm not exploit decreasing cost activities (such as process Y_1) and expand there to become a monopoly? Because, says Stigler, at any given time in the life cycle of an industry 'these functions may be too small to support a specialised firm'. As an industry grows, however, the magnitude of the process Y_1 may become

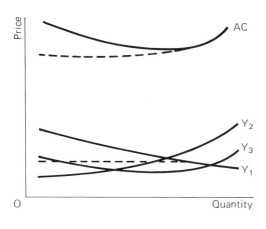

Diagram 2.1

sufficient to support a specialist firm. Existing firms will abandon Y_1 and a new firm will take it over. This abandonment of Y_1 will alter the cost curves of the original firms. Y_1 will be replaced by a horizontal line (the purchase price which equals the previous average cost of the process to the firms abandoning Y_1) and so the final product's total average cost curve (the vertical summation of Y_1, Y_2 and Y_3) will also change shape and position. The new industry, in its turn, may come to abandon parts of the process Y_1 to a new set of specialists.

As the industry contracts and the market is no longer available to support a specialist firm in process Y_1 the reverse procedure postulated by Stigler of reintegration will occur.

Processes such as Y_2 and Y_3 which are subject to

increasing costs can be handled in the conventional manner. There is no need for a firm to restrict its scale of operation in these functions. Stigler argues that part of the required amount can be made within the firm and the remainder purchased from outside suppliers. 'Outside' suppliers could, of course, include replicated optimal sized plants within the same firm.

(d) DIVISION OF LABOUR AND THE EMPIRICAL EVIDENCE

The division of labour is a concept which is as valid today as it was to Adam Smith's pinmakers. The engineer might regard this as self-evident at first glance. On re-examination he might think it less obvious. As Professor Stigler put it: 'Industry does not consist, and shows no marked tendency to consist of "hordes of men and women pouring into and out of 40-acre buildings".'[5] Tables 2.1, 2.2 and 2.3 provide data supporting this view for both the USA and the UK.

In the USA it is quite clear that over a long period there has been no increase in the average size of factories (measured by employment) and more than two-thirds of all workers in manufacturing were employed in factories with less than 1000 workers. In the UK the data, although less comprehensive for average size and size distribution, suggest

Table 2.1 Size of factories by employment, 1954–1972 (USA)

No. of employees per factory	Percentage of total manufacturing employment in each size group		
	1954	1963	1972
Up to 20	7.7	7.3	6.2
20–99	18.1	18.9	18.6
100–299	15.5	16.8	17.9
250–999	26.0	26.5	28.6
1000 and over	32.6	30.5	28.7
	100.0	100.0	100.0

Source: Statistical Abstract of the United States, 1975.

Table 2.2 Size of establishments in factory trades with more
more than 10 employees, 1952—1961 (UK)

	Average number of employees per establishment	Percentage of total employees in establishments with:	
		500 or less employees	2000 or more employees
1952	127	54.9	19.0
1955	140	52.0	20.6
1959	139	52.7	20.6
1961	148	51.3	21.3

Source: Ministry of Labour Gazatte

Table 2.3 Manufacturing industries: Average size of
all establishments, 1958—1968 (UK)

	Average number of employees per establishment
1958	83.9
1963	88.4
1968	86.8

Source: Census of Production, 1958 and 1968.

that there was some increase in size after 1952, but very
little since 1955. The average factory employs less than
100 employees and at least one half of all workers in
manufacturing are employed in factories with less than
500 workers.*

Lest it be thought that these data, by restricting the
discussion to establishments or factories, distort the
conclusions by ignoring any scale economies available to
the multi-plant firm (in finance, marketing, risk and
management) tables 2.4, 2.5 and 2.6 relate to firms. Table
2.4 shows that in the US the proportion of total output
attributed to the 50 or 100 largest manufacturing firms
remained virtually unchanged from 1954 onwards.

Table 2.5 moves away from the generality of table 2.4
which related to the total economy. Here the share of the

---

* For a fuller discussion of these points see J. Jewkes, *Delusions
of Dominance*, Institute of Economic Affairs 1977.

Table 2.4 Share of value added of the largest US corporations in manufacturing 1954—72

	Largest 50 (%)	Largest 100 (%)
1954	23	30
1958	23	30
1963	25	33
1966	25	33
1967	25	33
1970	24	33
1972	25	33

Source: Statistical Abstract of the United States, 1975

Table 2.5 Share by value of shipments by the four largest corporations in 43 US industries 1963—72

Percentage share of shipments by 4 largest companies	Number of industries		
	1963	1967	1972
90 per cent and over	2	1	1
70—89 per cent	4	5	5
50—69 per cent	5	3	4
30—49 per cent	11	12	13
under 30 per cent	21	22	20
Total	43	43	43

Source: Statistical Abstract of the United States, 1975

Table 2.6 Proportion of total employment in UK industries with 'high' concentration ratios, 1935—63

	Number of industries in samples	Number of industries with 'high' concentration ratios	3-firm or 4-firm concentration ratio	Employment in (2) as % of employment in (1)
	(1)	(2)	(3)	(4)
1935	233	31	3-firm	6.5
1951	211	36	3-firm	7.9
1958	117	11	4-firm	3.4
1963	117	14	4-firm	5.1

Source: S. Aaronovitch and M.C. Sawyer, 'The concentration of British manufacturing industry', Lloyds Bank Review 1974

largest four companies in each of 43 US industries is examined. There is no evidence there that the presence of scale economies is moving the industries towards the 'logical' monopoly outcome. A similar conclusion is obtained from table 2.6, relating to the British economy. Despite the different census bases from which the table is derived, and the switch from three- to four-firm concentration ratios (defining 'high' concentration industries as those industries where 70% or more of all workers are employed in the largest three or four firms) there is nothing to suggest a movement towards a 'logical organisation of industry'.

This does not mean that the premises underlying the division of labour are invalid, however. The extent to which monopolisation of any particular final or intermediate product market is possible depends, as Stigler and Smith pointed out, on whether or not that market is large enough to support such a specialised firm. It is dependent on whether or not consumers want the product produced by the specialist. If they do not, the specialist firm will not emerge and more integrated firms will continue to operate at apparently sub-optimal scales. When and if consumers do want such products in sufficient quantities at given prices specialist firms will appear. When consumers cease to want these products in sufficient quantities at the relevant prices then the monopoly of the specialist will vanish as its operations are absorbed again by one of the firms operating at some other stage in the productive process.

Given product differentiation and varying consumer tastes, and given that both of these alter over time, any monopoly based on the (valid) principle of the division of labour will be short-lived. 'The top is a very slippery place', as a study by Professors Hymer and Pashigan confirmed. They examined the 1000 largest manufacturing firms in the USA from 1946–55. The firms were categorised by industry. Instead of finding 'greater market share stability in the more concentrated industries, ... the contrary appears true'. More specifically, table 2.7 gives illustrations from three industries in the USA showing how there is a

Table 2.7 Percentage distribution of total assets, chemicals, steel and motor vehicles, USA, various years

Chemicals	1909	1919	1929	1935	1948	1960	1968
Du Pont	75	51	46	53	41	37	25
Union Carbide	—	37	28	25	25	20	24
General Allied Chemical	25	13	26	23	12	10	11
Dow Chemical	—	—	—	—	10	12	18
American Cyanamid	—	—	—	—	7	8	7
Monsanto	—	—	—	—	6	13	14
Total	100	100	100	100	100	100	100

Steel	1909	1919	1929	1935	1948	1960	1968
US Steel Corporation	91	77	54	51	45	39	39
Republic	4	4	8	8	9	9	10
Bethlehem	3	12	19	19	18	18	19
Jones & Laughlin	2	4	5	5	7	6	—
National	—	—	3	5	6	7	8
Inland Steel	—	—	2	3	5	7	7
Am. Rolling Mill	—	—	3	3	6	8	10
Youngtown Sheet	—	4	6	6	5	6	6
Total	100	100	100	100	100	100	100

Motor Vehicles	1919	1929	1935	1948	1960	1968
General Motors	48	55	63	64	61	50
Ford	36	31	29	25	29	32
Chrysler	—	9	8	12	10	16
Packard	7	—	—	—	—	—
Studebaker	9	6	—	—	—	—
Total	100	100	100	100	100	100

Source: A.D.H. Kaplan, 'Big enterprise in a competitive system', Fortune Directory.

tendency for firms which have gained a dominant position to lose ground relatively, if not absolutely. (The data relating to motor vehicles in particular would have provided a still more obvious indication of this had they related to market shares by sales and not total domestically owned assets: imports from Japan and Europe have substantially increased the degree of rivalry in the American car industry and this is not reflected in manufacturing assets.) Table 2.8 provides not dissimilar information for three British industries.

Table 2.8 Percentage distribution of market share by volume: Cigarettes, Washing Products, Retail Petrol, UK, various years

Cigarettes	1958	1959	1960	1961	1962	1963	1964
Imperial	70	65½	61½	59	58	57½	56½
Gallaher	24¼	28	30¾	32½	37	37	37
Carreras	2	3	3¼	3¾	4½	5¼	6
Others	3¾	3½	4½	5	½	½	½
	100	100	100	100	100	100	100

	1965	1966	1967	1968	1969	1970
Imperial	57	62¼	65½	66¼	66	67½
Gallaher	36	31	27¾	27¼	27¼	25¼
Carreras	6¾	6¼	6½	6½	6¾	7
Others	½	¼	¼	¼	¼	¼
	100	100	100	100	100	100

Source: The Growth of Competition, Industrial Policy Group, 1970

Washing Products	1921	1924	1929	1935	1938	1954	1964
Lever Bros. (later Unilever)	67	62	60	54	52	53	46
Thos. Hedley (later Procter & Gamble)	Neg	Neg	1	8	14	30	34
CWS	11	10	12	10	11	6	3
Others	22	28	27	28	23	11	17
	100	100	100	100	100	100	100

Source: George Polanyi: 'Detergents: A question of monopoly?', Institute of Economic Affairs, 1970, p. 74.

Retail Petrol	1953	1960	1964	1972
Shell-Mex and BP	51.4	49.4	45.0	38.2
Esso	28.4	29.8	27.4	20.0
Regent/Texaco	14.0	12.5	11.1	8.4
Mobil	1.1	4.2	5.9	7.6
Petrofina	2.2	2.5	2.5	2.5
Continental (including Jet)	–	0.7	3.5	4.3
Burmah	–	–	0.4	2.0
V.I.P.	–	–	0.8	3.0
Total	–	–	1.0	3.0
Others	2.9	0.9	2.4	10.8
	100.0	100.0	100.0	100.0

Source: R.W. Shaw and C.J. Sutton, Industry and Competition, Macmillan 1976, p. 24.

Division of labour as Florence, Kaldor and Robinson noted, has not led to monopoly. From an engineering viewpoint this is 'illogical'. In a static situation division of labour, as Kaldor pointed out, must lead to monopolistic industries. Robinson's view that coordination is a function subject to some form of diminishing returns is apparently plausible as a rationale for the existence of optimum firms below monopoly size. But given that he restricts the coordination task to problems faced only *within* the firm it does not explain why industries do not further subdivide themselves by technological processes so that the resulting (monopolistic) firms would be sufficiently small not to exceed that threshold level where average in-firm coordination costs begin to rise. Stigler argued (and provided empirical evidence supporting his view) that industries *do* become vertically disintegrated as demand increases, and reintegrated as demand decreases. The market is dynamic not static. Robinson's coordination costs need not limit size of firm relative to industry, given an appropriate definition of 'industry'. Some tasks can be carried out within the firm, and others can be hived off and carried out for the firm in other industries as the original firm exercises its rights in the market place as buyer or seller of product inputs and outputs.

Division of labour is a consequence not a cause. It is the consequence of Smith's 'invisible hand' whereby buyers and sellers 'truck, barter and exchange'. If a more profitable trade can be engaged in by specialisation, specialisation will result. Division of labour is not the cause of a 'logical' industrial organisation. A logical industrial organisation is that which maximises the net benefits of buyers, sellers and entrepreneurs. It may, but probably will not, be reflected in monopoly control of the market, as judged by broadbrush census of production figures, persisting over time. It need not, but more probably will, be reflected in a unique matching of individual consumer wants with individual producer outputs. (This is not the same as perfect competition, where wants and outputs are not unique but are homogeneous.)

This assertion that many trade exchanges are 'unique' can be made because consumer tastes and production possibilities vary enormously not only over time, but also at any one point in time. All individuals differ to a greater or lesser degree. Producers, similarly, cannot be bracketed neatly into the 'rubber industry', or the 'washing product industry' or whatever. For example, Stigler and Kindahl[7] calculated that the steel industry can produce hot rolled carbon steel sheets with so many attributes that there are theoretically 135 million varieties, and the varieties produced in any one year must be immense. (This ignores bar, strip and plate steel.) Even one single manufacturer[8] of nuts, bolts, screws and other fasteners and related products, Guest, Keen and Nettlefolds Ltd, produces in its appropriate divisions 11,500 million pieces annually and offers 35,000 different items of various sizes, qualities and material. Table 2.9 lists the wide variety of synthetic rubbers which are available. Table 2.10 shows how, over the period 1947—69 consumer choice increased in the home laundry products market. The number of alternative products available more than tripled. And the widened range of choice is probably even greater than these figures suggest since many products would be introduced to the market but would be subsequently withdrawn when lack of sales success made it apparent that they were failing to meet changing market demand. Table 2.11 shows how this increased choice owed little or nothing to the awarding of different brand names by the same manufacturer to the same basic product. Each principal firm produced one main product to satisfy one particular type of consumer want.

Thus at a disaggregated level many exchanges are possibly unique. They could not have been made with alternative suppliers or consumers without some loss of satisfaction to either purchaser or producer. To the extent that that is true, much more industry is 'monopolised' than broad-brush census studies indicate. But it is because producers and consumers see opportunities to trade profitably with each other that such large varieties of

Table 2.9 List of types and grades of synthetic rubbers

A Styrene-Butadiene and Butadiene Rubbers	No of grades
a Emulsion polymerised	
i Hot — non-pigmented dry	37
ii Cold — non-pigmented dry	43
— black masterbatch dry	33
— oil masterbatch dry	48
— oil/black masterbatch dry	55
iii Resin rubber masterbatch dry	30
iv Latices	194
b Solution polymerised	
i Butadiene dry	51
ii Styrene-butadiene dry	26
	517
B Isoprene solution polymerised	
i Isoprene dry	15
ii Isoprene latex	1
C Ethylene-propylene Rubbers	66
D Butyl Rubbers	43
E Polychloroprene Rubbers	
i Dry	47
ii Latices	23
F Nitrile Rubbers	
i Normal	228
ii Vinyl modified	39
iii Latices	110
Total	**1,089**

Source: International Institute of Synthetic Rubber Producers, 1970

Table 2.10 Home laundry products number of choices
(by brand, type and size)

	1947	1969	
Soap flakes	30	86	Soap flakes, powders,
and detergents			powdered detergents
	0	75	Liquid detergents
	0	5	Enzyme powders
Household soap	28	14	Household soap
Dry Starch	14	34	Starches
Liquid bleaches	20	60	Bleaches
	0	8	Fabric softners
	0	6	Pre-wash soakers
Total	92	288	Total

Source: Nielsen Researcher, 1970

Table 2.11 Principal brands of Unilever and Procter & Gamble Ltd in the heavy duty detergent powder market, 1975

Type	Unilever	Procter and Gamble
Soap	Persil	Fairy Snow
Synthetic Detergent	Omo	Daz
Cut-price Detergent	Surf	Tide
Low Lathering Synthetic	Persil Automatic	Bold
Enzyme	Radiant	Ariel

generically similar goods are demanded and supplied. Such monopolies and monopsonies, however, are not discernible in statistical aggregates. More importantly, they may not persist beyond one or a few exchanges.

If such trades are voluntarily negotiated and, at the time of negotiation, neither party perceives the possibility of superior exchanges, then these trades and the industrial organisation within which they take place can be regarded as optimal.

To increase the concentration of industry as defined by census takers (which has been the policy of successive British governments over the years)* may appear to be 'logical' but it may not be 'optimal' as defined here. Is then the reverse procedure (favoured by many American policy makers) of encouraging industrial deconcentration more sensible? Like the 'logic' of concentration a case can be made out for deconcentration using standard economic theory. But, like the 'logic' of large size (based erroneously on the principle of division of labour), the rationale for deconcentration (based on the theory of perfect competition) has, as we shall see in the next two chapters, no better foundation.

REFERENCES

1 P. Sargant Florence, *Logic of Industrial Organisation*, Routledge and Kegan Paul, 1933. pp. 260—1.

---

* For example, industry nationalisation, induced rationalisation of industries such as textiles and ship building and encouragement of mergers via the Industrial Reorganisation Corporation and the National Enterprise Board.

2   N. Kaldor, 'The equilibrium of the firm', *Economic Journal* 1934.
3   E.A.G. Robinson, 'The problem of management and the size of firm', *Economic Journal* 1934.
4   G.J. Stigler, 'The division of labour is limited by the extent of the market', *Journal of Political Economy* 1951.
5   G.J. Stigler, *Trends in Output and Employment*, National Bureau for Economic Research (NBER), 1949, p. 38.
6   S. Hymer and P. Pashigian, 'Turnover of firms as a measure of market behaviour', *Review of Economics and Statistics* 1962.
7   G.J. Stigler and J.K. Kindahl, *The Behaviour of Industrial Prices*, NBER, 1970, pp. 4–5.
8   *The Growth of Competition*, Industrial Policy Group, 1970, p. 10.

. . . established firms will increase their output . . .
until their marginal and average costs are equal to
their selling prices. Entry is not requisite . . .
since the ability of all firms to expand . . . without
exceeding minimal costs . . . plus the independent
pricing attributable to atomism, lead to the
result even without entry.

Joe S Bain
Barriers to New Competition, 1956.

3

The Structure / Conduct / Performance Paradigm

The standard neo-classical market structure model stretches from monopoly through oligopoly and monopolistic competition. The implication is that at one end of the monopoly/perfect-competition continuum competition is zero and at the other end it is maximised. It has already been argued in Chapter 1 that this is a misleading framework. Indeed the model altogether ignores the verb 'to compete' and the competitive process. The competitive process is that force which determines actual price in the market place and which aids the achievement of allocative efficiency by forcing successive transaction prices ever closer to equivalence with marginal cost. This (classical) view has no place in the neo-classical equilibrium of perfect competition. In perfectly competitive equilibrium each transaction price equals marginal cost and allocative efficiency already obtains. The similarity in wording for these two definitions of process and equilibrium respectively, goes a long way to explaining why the classical approach has been neglected. The analytic elegance which can be attributed to a state of

equilibrium *vis à vis* a dynamic process means that mathematical techniques rather than verbal logic can be apparently
and easily applied to economic problems. This factor,
coupled with the increasing use of mathematics in economics, has meant that the more meaningful classical approach
has suffered the fate of neglect. This chapter continues this
neglect and details the neo-classical model. It examines its
deficiencies as a prescriptive instrument. Chapter 4 shows
how the structure/conduct/performance paradigm also
fails to be an adequate predictor of industrial behaviour
and performance. These flaws will then be contrasted in
Chapters 5, 6 and 7 with the more successful approach of
analysing the roles of the entrepreneur and of exchange.
This, it will be discovered, is both conceptually more appeal-
ing and empirically more valid. Meanwhile, the conventional view of industrial economics and perfect competition
will be examined and appraised.

(a) THE MEANING AND IMPORTANCE OF PRICE

The importance of price derives from the Marshallian
theory of value and the idea of consumer surplus. These
rest on the basic postulate of demand that the lower the
price of a good, the more of it any group of consumers will
purchase. This relationship is embodied in the market
demand curve for the good. The demand function contains
information about the value consumers attach to their use
of the good in question. As the price is lowered either
existing consumers increase consumption and/or new
consumers commence to purchase the good for the first
time.

In a system where the concept of consumers' sovereignty
is meaningful the demand curve for a good shows the net
social benefits which can be obtained from consumption
of that good (geometrically these are represented by the
consumer surplus triangle). At the margin market price is
the reservation price of the marginal consumer. It is that
price just low enough to overcome his reservations about

purchasing an extra unit. It indicates in monetary terms how much an incremental unit is worth to him. (In equilibrium price = marginal utility, provided marginal utility is modified by dividing it by the marginal utility of money.)

(b) THE EFFICIENCY OF PERFECT COMPETITION*

What distinguishes perfect competition from monopoly and monopolistic competition? The unique answer is that only in perfect competition is price equated with marginal cost. In addition, in perfect competition price equals average cost and does so at a minimum. Thus there are no supra-normal profits and the output level is where productive efficiency is maximised. But equity (in terms of an absence of monopoly or supra-normal profits) is also present in the Chamberlinian tangency situation; and it is possible for a nonopolist to construct a plant which has a short-run average cost curve tangential to the horizontal portion of an L-shaped or flat-bottom U-shaped long-run average cost curve, and so to operate at optimal size. Diagram 3.1 illustrates these three alternatives. The only *unique* attribute of perfect competition is $P = MC$.

Why, to cite Scherer, is the condition of $P > MC$ the 'basis of the economist's most general condemnation of monopoly'? How does it lead to 'an allocation of resources which is inefficient in the sense of satisfying consumer wants with less than maximum effectiveness'?[1] Consider diagram 3.2 where the only two industries in a hypothetical economy are depicted. X is a monopoly, Y is perfectly competitive. (The axes scales for X and Y are not identical.)

If a price of £10 is charged for a unit of X (profit maximising $MR = MC$) only 2 million units will be produced. Consumers who consider a unit of X is worth £9.99 but no more than that will be excluded from the market. But such

---

* The arguments of this and the final two sections of this chapter draw on those elaborated in the first five chapters of F.M. Scherer, *Industrial Structure and Economic Performance*, Rand McNally, 1970.

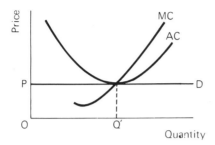

(a) Perfect competition

P = MC
P = AC
Q at minimum AC

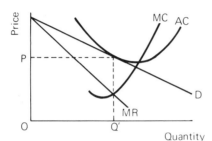

(b) Monopolistic competition

P > MC
P = AC
Q < minimum AC

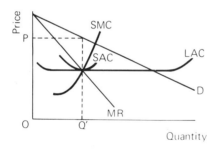

(c) Monopoly

P > MC
P > AC
Q at minimum AC

Diagram 3.1

an extra unit worth £9.99 can be produced with resources costing only £5. That is, marginal social value exceeds marginal social costs, and this inequality would continue through to an output of 4 million units where $P = MC$.

Given full employment, the resources necessary to produce an extra unit of X must come from industry Y. In Y output is 50 million units, price is £4. Now transfer an insignificant but positive amount of resources from Y to X, say £20 in monetary terms. Four extra units of X would be produced for £5 per unit and sold for (say) £9.99. A

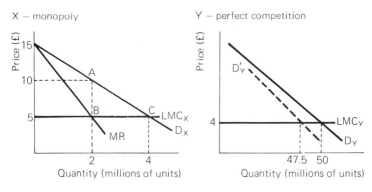

Diagram 3.2

social gain of $(4 \times £9.99) - £20 = £19.96$ would be realised in X. In Y five units would be forgone due to the £20 reduction in resources. Y's price might have to be raised to £4.01 to avoid the presence of unsatisfied willing buyers at a selling price of £4. A social cost of $(5 \times £4.01) - £20 = £0.05$ would be realised in Y. A net social gain of £19.91 would be realised by this transfer of resources from Y towards X.

Thus in a situation like diagram 3.2 there is inefficient allocation of resources. Too few are being utilised by the monopolist and too many by the perfect competitor. If X can be transformed in some way into a perfectly competitive industry this inefficiency would cease to exist. If the profits to be made in X attract entrepreneurs from Y resources will be shifted from Y to X. The price of X will fall to clear the increased output. D_y will be shifted down and to the left to D'_y as a result of the substitution effect (some people now buy X who previously bought Y). £10 million of resources will shift to X in order to increase output to 4 million units. This resource shift will increase social output from X (as valued by consumers) by £10 million $(4 \times 2.5$ million$)$, resulting in a net social gain of ABC, the original deadweight loss which resulted from the monopolistic behaviour of industry X.

At this point a resource transfer in either direction will represent a net loss to society.

(c) SHOULD GOVERNMENT EDICT COMPEL THE
EXISTENCE OF PERFECT COMPETITION?

The apparent answer to the above question would be in the affirmative (if optimal resource allocation is the objective of society). Our discussion of perfect competition would seem to indicate that it results in an optimal pricing pattern provided it holds in each and every industry. The actual answer must be in the negative. One main reason is that in many industries scale economies are present and over a range larger firms have lower costs than smaller. Then monopoly or oligopoly may more closely approximate to the 'ideal' (i.e. social welfare maximisation) than would perfect competition. Consider diagram 3.3 where economies of scale are reflected in the lower level of a constant cost function.

DD is the industry demand curve for a homogeneous product. LMC_0 is the minimum attainable long-run average and marginal cost curve. Assume it can only exist when firms are so large that the industry is oligopolistic. LMC_c is the equivalent cost schedule if the industry was atomistic in structure and perfectly competitive in behaviour.* P_c is the price which would rule in the latter conditions. P_0 can conceivably be the same as, lower than, or higher than the competitive $(P = MC)$ price. These three alternatives are indicated in the diagram.

When $P_c = P_0$, consumer surplus is *abc* for either market structure. The consumer is as well off under either, but the producer is better off by profits amounting to *bcde*. Unless the object of government is simply to punish producers

---

* In strict perfectly competitive theory firms are assumed to be of optimal size, thus the two LMC curves would *not* be unequal. However, in industries where firms are in fact of optimal size they may then be so few in number that oligopoly obtains and the firms no longer price at MC. To illustrate why or why not a statutory industrial concentration or deconcentration policy is desirable the assumption is made here that the cost curves *do* differ. In the next sub-section the converse assumption is made: that firms *are* permitted to expand to optimal size but are then required to price at (optimal) LMC.

Competitive price equal to oligopoly price

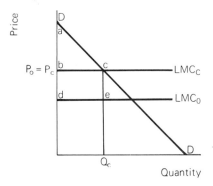

Competitive price above oligopoly price   Competitive price below oligopoly price

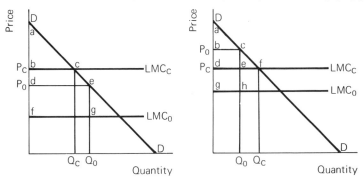

Diagram 3.3

there is no reason to compel perfect competition. Society would lose by such a change in industrial structure. (Society consists of *both* consumers and producers.)

When price under oligopoly is below LMC_c then consumers' surplus increases to *ade* from *abc* and producers' surplus rises from zero to *defg*. Again it is hard to justify compulsion of perfect competition. The third case is more complex, however. When prices under oligopoly are higher than P_c even though costs are lower we have what Williamson termed the trade-off case.[2] Consumer surplus would be larger under competition by an amount equal to *bcdef*, but profits are larger under oligopoly by amount *bcgh*. Under oligopoly, in overall social terms the amount *bcde* cancels; it is gained by producers and lost by consumers. The amount *abc* is common to both situations. The overall issue is whether the sum of 'net' profits due to technical efficiency under oligopoly is greater than the resulting deadweight allocative loss. The trade-off is *degh* against *cef*. Before recommending perfect competition this trade-off must be made even though price is assumed higher than marginal cost would be in an atomistic situation.

Even in this latter instance, a negative answer to our original question can be given. Williamson's trade-off theory, as McGee has pointed out, ignores entry.[3] Provided that entry to the industry is not barred, any firm which can achieve cost conditions of LMC_c will be attracted to enter the industry if price is P_0. This will ultimately force price down from P_0 to P_c. In the short run the size of *cef* will be reduced, making the trade-off appear more favourable. In the long run *cef* will be eliminated completely leaving only the two cases of $P_c = P_0$ or $P_c > P_0$.

(d) SHOULD GOVERNMENT EDICT COMPEL THE PRACTICE OF PRICING AT LONG-RUN MARGINAL COST?

This question may at once be both more practical and more meaningful than whether or not the fragmented industrial structure of perfect competition should be fostered everywhere in the economy. The main attraction of perfect competition is, after all, not its atomistic structure but its outcome of $P = MC$. Moreover, if industries are not permitted to take advantage of scale economies the result, as we have seen, is that scarce social resources which could have been used elsewhere are diverted towards producing commodities at a higher unit cost than is necessary.

At least two problems discourage the provision of an affirmative answer to this question. First, there is the difficulty of how to recoup total costs from the market place when scale economies have still to be exhausted. Second, there is the problem of non-allocable joint costs which must also somehow be recouped from the market

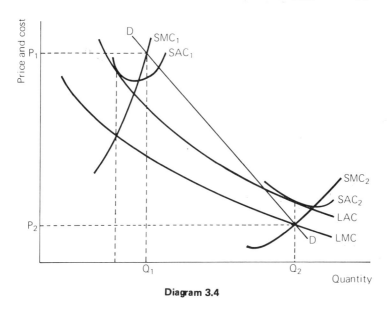

Diagram 3.4

but which cannot be attributed directly to any particular product.

Diagram 3.4 is the standard model used to show the optimal price and output position for a decreasing cost industry. With plant size SAC_1, pricing at SMC results in a profit earning P_1Q_1 price–output combination. But $SMC > LMC$ at P_1Q_1 and economic welfare will only be maximised when investment takes place and a plant size with a cost structure of SAC_2 is attained.* Then $P = SMC = LMC$, but although welfare is then maximised the firm is making a loss. Subsidies and two-part tariffs are practical methods which have been suggested by which industries can meet such deficits. Inevitably, however, such techniques also distort resource allocation. Marginal

---

* If at $P = SMC$ and $SMC > LMC$, then if price is reduced from P_1 to P_2 and output increased from Q_1 to Q_2, the marginal social benefits of expansion are equal to ½ $(P_2 + P_1)(Q_2 - Q_1)$ or ½ $(SMC_2 + SMC_1)(Q_2 - Q_1)$, i.e. the short-run marginal costs of expansion. The marginal social costs of expansion are k (incremental capital cost) plus r $(Q_2 - Q_1)$, where r is unit operating costs. The optimal expansion of an industry should continue until marginal social benefits (SMC) equal marginal social costs (LMC).

consumers may be deterred by a flat fee at the margin although quite willing to pay their reservation price. Equity may be disturbed unless those subsidised also contribute the tax revenue from which the subsidy is paid. The ideal solution (if it was costless to implement) is for each person to pay the same price at the margin $(P = MC)$ and for the deficit to be made up by each consumer somehow accepting a share of it according to the valuation he places on intra-marginal units as indicated by the consumer's surplus of his own unique demand curve. This whole topic has spawned a proliferation of literature which was summarised by Webb.[4] None of the various practical 'solutions' to the problem, however, approach the apparent ideal of a perfectly competitive equilibrium.

This problem is unique to decreasing cost industries. The second problem, that of common costs, is similar in complexity and is present in virtually all productive activity. The price of any product must exceed its marginal cost of production in order to contain its own assignable overhead costs and also that portion of common costs allocated to it both apportioned over the quantity of the product sold. How great should this excess be? And how should it vary product by product?

If we accept the non-Austrian, neo-classical view that all commodities should be priced at long-run marginal cost, common costs should be allocated in such a way as to minimise the social losses which arise due to the resulting higher prices and so reduced consumption. In discrete terms this will be achieved when the following relationship holds between any two commodities:

$$\frac{\text{MSB}_1}{\text{DWL}_1} = \frac{\text{MSB}_2}{\text{DWL}_2} \tag{1}$$

where the subscripts denote the products, and MSB and DWL respectively indicate the incremental social benefits forgone as valued by the marginal consumer and the deadweight loss incurred as a consequence of the relevant common costs being added to the perfectly competitive price of each product. The equality can be rewritten as:

$$\frac{Z_1}{Z_2} = \frac{DWL_1}{DWL_2} \qquad (2)$$

where Z denotes the price-production cost mark-up for each product. That is $Z = \Delta P$, where ΔP is the mark-up required to cover pro-rated common costs above the original competitive price, $P = MC$. Optimality then, occurs when the social benefits from all products as measured by the market's willingness to pay the price premium are equal at the margin per pound of deadweight loss necessarily forgone to cover common costs (subject to the constraint that total incremental revenue, $\Sigma_{i=1}^{2} R_i$, is constant and equal to common costs).

The implications of this relationship can be intuitively understood by reference to diagram 3.5a, which is similar to that first used by Baumol and Bradford.[5] Products 1 and 2 have demand curves $D_1 D_1$ and $D_2 D_2$ respectively.

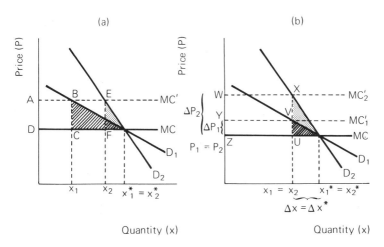

Demand curves for products with differing price elasticities.
(Prices set to reflect differing mark-ups.)

Note: Prices are set so that:

ABCD + AEFD = WXUZ + YVUZ

i.e. so that total incremental revenue equals common costs.

Diagram 3.5

In both cases marginal production costs equal MC. If the share of common costs allocated to each product is the same then MC rises to MC' and the original competitive output levels of $x_1{}^* = x_2{}^*$ fall to x_1 and x_2. The respective deadweight losses are given by the shaded and by the dotted regions. It is clear that minimisation of the aggregate deadweight losses implies that products with a relatively price elastic demand should bear a relatively smaller share of common costs than those with an inelastic demand, other things equal.

Prices should be set in such a way that the proportionate change in output from the original competitive levels should be the same for all products, irrespective of market size. This can be shown diagrammatically at the expense only of some generalisation. Diagram 3.5b is restricted to the same two-product case, and equivalent competitive output levels of $x_1{}^* = x_2{}^*$ and MC levels of $P_1 = P_2$ are assumed. Total incremental revenue required to cover common costs, $\Sigma_{i=1}^{2} R_i$, is ABCD + AEFD (as indicated in diagram 3.5a). In the optimal situation $\Sigma_{i=1}^{2} R_i$ must be constant and equation (1) satisfied. Thus ABCD + AEFD must equal WXUZ + YVUZ in diagram 3.5b. Clearly, the sum of the deadweight losses (the dotted plus the shaded triangles) is less in diagram 3.5b. No other pricing policy would result in a smaller aggregate deadweight loss. It can readily be inferred that the optimal allocation of common costs is such that P_1 and P_2 should be raised by ΔP_1 and ΔP_2 respectively, and output should be reduced by the equal proportions $\Delta x = \Delta x^*$.

To prove this, assume that the price elevations are sufficiently small so that elasticities are constant over the relevant range. Then:

$$\text{DWL}_1 = \tfrac{1}{2}\, \Delta P_1 . \Delta x_1 \qquad\qquad (3)$$

But elasticity of demand for product 1, $e_1 = P_1 . \Delta x_1 / x_1{}^* . \Delta P_1$. So:

$$\Delta P_1 = P_1 \Delta x_1 / x_1^* e_1 \qquad (4)$$

Now substitute (4) in (3):

$$\text{DWL}_1 = \frac{1}{2}(P_1 \Delta x_1{}^2)/x_1^* e_1 \qquad (5)$$

A similar expression can be calculated for DWL_2. Now insert into the optimality requirements (2) and we obtain:

$$\frac{Z_1}{Z_2} = \frac{P_1 \Delta x_1^2 \, x_2^* \, e_2}{P_2 \Delta x_2^2 \, x_1^* e_1} = \frac{e_2}{e_1} \, . \qquad (6)$$

This result, $Z_1/Z_2 = e_2/e_1$, the 'inverse elasticity formula', confirms the implication arrived at earlier, that the more inelastic the demand for the product, the greater should be the percentage deviation from marginal cost. To cite Baumol and Bradford, the price of each product should be set so that 'its percentage deviation from marginal cost is inversely proportional to the item's price elasticity of demand'.

This socially optimal pricing rule is unlikely to be followed by any regulatory agency. The informational requirements are too exacting, and precise cost and demand schedules for all products cannot be known to the authorities. Without such information, attempts at imposing optimal pricing behaviour would be futile. Even if that data were available it is doubtful if any quasi-political pricing body with discretionary power would employ them in the optimal manner. High-demand elasticity generally means ready availability of substitutes. Low-demand elasticity, conversely, tends to mean that people who want a certain product have few alternatives available to them and/or regard the product as a 'necessity'. When this is the case they would be likely to raise considerable and vocal objections to a relatively high price for such a product. The monolithic political mechanism, unlike the more pluralistic commercial market, works in such a way that overt pressure group objections of this kind tend to be deferred to, irrespective of their overall social merits.

Gordon Tullock has emphasised that governments can 'fail' just as markets can 'fail'. In his paper 'The Vote Motive'* he writes:

> In the real world, voters frequently are much more interested in one issue than another: . . . Anyone who has observed real politicians in action sees how they solve the problem. They try to give to minority groups with strong preferences in one item . . . favourable treatment in (that item), and then hope that the group will accept relatively unfavourable treatment in other issues where its feelings are less intense . . . this analysis of the politician's tactics indicates simply that he is attempting to be re-elected to office, not that he is attempting to maximise the public interest.

In short, where there is (and in reality there *always* is) market failure *and* government failure the issue crystallises around which form of organisation is the least bad.† It is not relevant to ask which organisation is 'perfect' under certain restrictions and unrealistic assumptions. Nirvana is unobtainable this side of the grave.

How does the (imperfect) market react to situations of the kind under discussion, namely the recovery of joint costs?

An unregulated profit maximising firm will adopt a pricing scheme at least qualitatively similar to the socially optimal one. In the short run overhead costs will be regarded by the firm as sunk, and the firm will then set $MR = MC$ for all products. Given that $MR_i = P_i (1 + 1/e_i)$ for any product i, where P_i is selling price including mark-up and given that $Z_i = (P_i - MC_i)/MC_i$ then with profit maximisation:

$$MR = MC$$

$$\text{So} \quad P(1 + \frac{1}{e}) = \frac{P - MC}{Z} = \frac{P - MR}{Z}$$

$$\text{and} \quad \frac{P(1 + e)}{e} = \left[P - \frac{P(1 + e)}{e} \right] \bigg/ Z$$

---

* Institute of Economic Affairs, 1976, p. 24.

† See also the discussion 'Second best' below.

cancelling and multiplying through by e we have

$$1 + e = -1/Z$$

Thus in a two-product profit maximising firm, prices are set so that for products 1 and 2:

$$\frac{1 + e_1}{1 + e_2} = \frac{Z_2}{Z_1} \tag{7}$$

which is not dissimilar to equation (6).

A commercial firm does not operate under the political constraints on economic good sense which a regulatory agency does. It can, therefore, pursue this type of pricing policy. It will not, of course, any more than a government body, have the requisite information to take such pricing decisions. The critical factor, however, is not the different levels of information available to each but rather their differing motivations. 'Under a wide range of circumstances individual firms behave as if they were seeking rationally to maximise their expected returns ... (with) full knowledge of the data needed to succeed in this attempt; *as if,* that is, they knew the relevant cost and demand functions.'[6] Whether the firm has or has not that information is irrelevant. If it behaves as though it had, then the underlying theory of equation (7) and the resulting implications for social and economic welfare are just as meaningful and valuable as they would be were profit maximising behaviour an accurate description of reality.[7]

A regulatory agency then, may take politically popular decisions on price which are economically and socially unsound. A profit maximising firm, conversely, will take pricing decisions which are not dissimilar to the economic and social optimum but which, if subject to political scrutiny, may appear unacceptable and unjustifiable.

Even if one could generously assume that a central pricing authority set prices according to inverse elasticities, firms would still not behave in an optimal manner. The reason is that recoupment of common overhead costs would be guaranteed *ex post* by regulation and by the necessary price adjustment. Only if common overhead costs could be predicted in advance and so the constraint $\Sigma_{i=1}^{2} R_i$ predetermined by regulation before outlay would the social optimum be achieved.

Lack of market discipline would then result in a regulated industry incurring unnecessary organisational slack. Overhead costs or corporate perquisites for staff above those required for running the business in the consumer interest would appear. The lesson is not that direct price regulation should be coupled with regulation of the minutiae of management activities. The point is that, even if price regulation were enlightened enough to follow the socially optimal formula, it would create long-run misallocation of overhead expenditures. To the extent that regulation fails to take elasticities into account then the case against it is strengthened.

(e) SHOULD GOVERNMENT EDICT INVOKE THE RULE OF PROPORTIONALITY?

Perfect competition is allegedly 'efficient' because, in equilibrium, price equals marginal cost. Yet perfect competition may be undesirable or unattainable because of the need for some industries to be composed of a few firms large enough to reap the benefits of scale economies. The prime attraction of perfect competition, however, is not its atomistic structure, but rather the $P = MC$ condition. Price equals marginal cost is a condition which in principle could be legally enforced but which in practice would result in efficiency and equity anomalies in declining cost indistries and similar anomalies in industries (almost all?) where common, non-allocable costs are present.

One other proposed route out of the theoretical morass and one which would still achieve a similar social optimum to marginal cost pricing is the rule of proportionality. This rule could enable industries or firms to charge a socially optimal price while still covering their costs. Thus for any two goods optimal pricing would require:

$$\frac{P_x}{MC_x} = \frac{P_y}{MC_y} \tag{8}$$

That this represents a social optimum can be seen by considering actual numbers. Say the relationship is

$$\frac{10}{5} = \frac{15}{7.5}$$

Then a shift of an insignificant amount of resources in a fully employed two-sector X and Y economy, such as £15 from Y to X will result in a gain of 3 units of X (selling at £10 each) and a loss of 2 units of Y (selling at £15 each). The position cannot be improved by resource reallocation.

Scherer[8] gives two main reasons why this rule would be unworkable in practice. First, the world would have to be composed entirely of *non-perfect* markets otherwise $P = MC$ would hold in the perfect markets. There is one fundamental market which cannot be rendered imperfect without at least some unacceptable degree of interference with individual liberty and that is the labour—leisure market. Second, the rule of proportionality only holds in an economy where all sales are made to final consumers not to intermediaries or reprocessors. In a complex economy this too is a virtually unattainable prerequisite.

Consider first the leisure market argument. The price of leisure is its opportunity cost. That is, it is the wage forgone in a perfect labour market, or it is that rate plus some premium in an imperfect market. For a situation where all markets are imperfect the price of leisure must be raised above its marginal cost to firms (i.e. the ruling wage rate) to that level where it has the same $P{:}MC$ ratio as is ruling in all other markets. This could be done if the government gave each member of society a subsidy per wage unit worked in order to raise the opportunity cost (the price) of leisure *vis à vis* the wage paid. This is manifestly impractical. But unless it were done leisure's low price would result in too small a supply of labour in a society where the rule of proportionality holds in every other market. Allocative efficiency would not be achieved, GNP would be too small, and over-much leisure would be consumed.

Now consider the second obstacle to enforcing the rule of proportionality. In an economy where some sales are not to final consumers but are made to intermediaries, then output is not maximised if the $P:MC$ ratio is identical in all markets. For example, say 100 kilograms of sugar can be produced from beet with 1 hour of labour costing £5. The sugar sells for £10, a $P:MC$ ratio of 2:1. In the brewing industry 1000 litres of beer also require 1 hour of labour costing £5, and 100 kilograms of sugar to aid fermentation, costing £10. The $P:MC$ rule suggests the beer should be sold for £30. But consumers buy both beer and sugar. Two hours of their labour can produce sugar valued at £20 or beer valued at £30. This suggests that labour should be reallocated away from sugar for final consumption towards beer (which will still require intermediate sugar). In this way the aggregate value of output will be raised, but the rule of proportionality will be violated.

(f) FROM ELEGANCE TO PRAGMATISM

Perfect competition may be undesirable because of the presence of scale economies. Marginal cost pricing appears to capture the benefits of perfect competition without incurring the costs of atomism. But the problems of decreasing cost industries and non-allocable common costs make universal marginal cost pricing an impractical and even an undesirable policy. Pricing in proportion to marginal costs provides results qualitatively similar to marginal cost pricing but this alternative is no less impractical given the presence of some markets which are and will always remain perfectly competitive, and of other markets which are for intermediate goods and not goods for final consumption.

These problems were tackled by Lipsey and Lancaster[9] in their theory of the second best. If first best ($P = MC$) solutions are unobtainable for the reasons detailed above, then can the relevant function (say GNP) be maximised subject to these constraints? In principle they answer positively. But, as Scherer[10] indicates, their 'general solutions are so complex that it is impossible to deduce unambiguously *even the direction* in which particular controlled prices should be adjusted'.

What then should be the role of the industrial economist when faced with such a counsel of despair? He can abandon the fight and leave the ring to politicians and others with normative, often non-quantifiable goals of national prestige, technological progress, income distribution, more or less socialism, and/or the competing interests of sectional groups of society. Alternatively he can attempt to obtain ever more sophisticated methods of applying marginal cost pricing rules in public utilities, and regulated or nationalised industries. Or he can make a subjective decision based on an assessment of (inconclusive) arguments that either more or less atomism or more or less concentration in industrial structure is a 'good thing'. Finally he could search for ways to make economic theory more meaningful to the policy makers, and if this implies some forfeiture of elegance this is a cost he should be prepared to bear.

The argument in this book leads inexorably towards the latter approach.

Chapter 4 deals with the empirical validity of adopting the former course of action. The structure/conduct/performance model as a base from which to argue towards more or less concentration in industrial structure is appraised. The results arrayed there will suggest that, quite apart from operational difficulties, a more cautious attitude should be adopted towards using neo-classical, perfectly competitive, theory as a policy guide.

REFERENCES

1   F.M. Scherer, *Industrial Structure and Economic Performance,* Rand McNally 1970.
2   O.E. Williamson, 'Economies as an antitrust defence', *American Economic Review* 1968.

3 J.S. McGee, *In Defence of Industrial Concentration*, Praeger 1971.

4 M.G. Webb, *Pricing Policies for Public Enterprises*, Macmillan 1976.

5 W.J. Baumol and R. Bradford, 'Optimal departures from marginal cost pricing', *American Economic Review* 1971.

6 Milton Friedman, *Essays in Positive Economics*, Chicago 1974, p. 21.

7 Friedman's billiard player example illustrates this argument brilliantly. 'Consider the problem of predicting the shots made by an expert billiard player. It seems not at all unreasonable that excellent predictions would be yielded by the hypothesis that the billiard player made his shots *as if* he knew the complicated mathematical formulae that would give the optimum directions of travel, could estimate accurately by eye the angles, etc., describing the location of the balls, could make lightning calculations from the formulae, and could then make the balls travel in the direction indicated by the formulae. Our confidence in this hypothesis is not based on the belief that billiard players, even expert ones, can or do go through the process described; it derives rather from the belief that unless in some way or other they were capable of reaching essentially the same result, they would not in fact be *expert* billiard players'. *(Essays in Positive Economics.)*

8 Scherer (1970).

9 R.G. Lipsey and K. Lancaster, 'The theory of the second best', *Review of Economic Studies* 1956.

10 Scherer (1970), p. 25.

*There must be outright dismantling of our gigantic
corporations and persistent prosecution of
producers who organise . . . for price maintenance
or output limitation . . . Legislation must
prohibit, and . . . prevent, . . . monopoly power,
regardless of how reasonably that power may appear
to be exercised.*

Henry C. Simons
Economic Policy for a Free Society, 1949.

4

Empirical Tests of the Market Concentration Doctrine

Perfectly competitive equilibrium is a state where an apparent form of socially optimal behaviour by firms exists. The situation may in reality be undesirable or unattainable but it has the virtue of a tractable and readily comprehensible theoretical base. In diagrammatic form it implies the following:

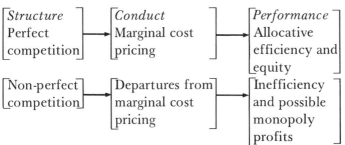

It is but a small step from a model of this kind to argue that monopoly profits will increase the more concentrated is the market. Bain[1] was among the first to spell out this relationship explicitly. He argued that successful collusion between firms would approach or result in joint profit maximisation. The ability to collude would increase with concentration and so, other things being equal, monopoly profit rates could be expected to increase with concentration as collusion became progressively more successful. (This statement, of course, rests on the implicit and unproven *assumption* that reaching and policing collusive agreements is cheaper when firms are fewer in number. If they are few, then this fact and *any* profits are viewed, possibly incorrectly, as proxies for the real economic problems of collusion and monopoly profits.)

In policy making circles both in the USA and UK these views are held. President Johnson's task force on the anti-trust laws called for a Concentrated Industries Act that would deconcentrate large industries in which four or fewer firms had an aggregate market share of 70% or more. This was needed because market concentration reduces 'the difficulty of maintaining collusive behaviour' and tends to produce 'effects equivalent to those of collusion ... even in the absence of collusion'.[2] (By the mid-1970s Senator Hart had introduced a Bill to Congress which proposed reducing the critical level of concentration to 50%.)

In the UK in 1973, the Government passed the Fair Trading Act which reduced from 33% to 25% the level of concentration required for a firm or group of firms to be regarded as a legal 'monopoly' for purposes of reference to the Monopolies and Mergers Commission. In that same year the Commission produced a report on 'the form of pricing behaviour likely to be found in industries where a major share ... is concentrated in the hands of a few large sellers'. The 'parallel pricing' which emerges is due to an appreciation by the firms 'that the interests of each ... might be best secured by the coordinated pursuit of the interests of the group as a whole'. In consequence there may be 'higher levels of prices and profits' and 'inflationary pressures in the economy may be exacerbated'.[3]

What empirical evidence is there to support the views that price—marginal-cost margins are greater in more concentrated industries? Is there any evidence to suggest that if such higher margins exist, then the desire of firms in concentrated industries to maximise joint profits will result in more frequent and larger price increases than would be the case in less concentrated industries? Does concentration even exacerbate the trade cycle as is implicit in the theory of the kinked demand curve?

(a) BAIN, STIGLER AND MANN

The premise that there is a link between concentration and monopoly profit rests largely on quantitative studies published during the 1950s and early 1960s, primarily using US data. Nearly all used data from the 1950s, excluding Bain's pioneering work which was based on figures drawn from the latter part of the 1930s. Bain selected 42 industries (from a total of 340) rejecting those where data was either unavailable or deemed to be unsuitable. Table 4.1 provides a summary of his major findings.

Bain could not and did not draw very firm conclusions from this investigation. A glance at the first two columns indicates that moderately concentrated industries earned lower rates of return on average than did highly concen-

Table 4.1 Average of industry average-profit rates, within concentration deciles, 42 selected industries 1936–40

Concentration ratio for 8 largest firms	Average of industry average-profit rate	Grouped average		No. of industries
90–100%	12.7%			8
80–89.9%	9.8%	11.8%	21	10
70–79.9%	16.3%			3
60–69.9%	5.8%			5
50–59.9%	5.8%			4
40–49.9%	8.6%			3
30–39.9%	6.3%	7.5%	21	5
20–29.9%	10.4%			2
10–19.9%	17.0%			1
0–9.9%	9.1%			1

Source: Bain[1] and Bain, 'Corrigendum', Quarterly Journal of Economics, 1951

trated ones, but they also earned lower profits than did industries of low concentration. However, dividing his sample into two halves, most and least concentrated, at the 70% level, he found a statistically significant difference between rates of return. This conclusion stimulated further research and did not disprove the theory that concentration and successful collusion are associated.

One study by Stigler,[4] although still more limited in scope than Bain's (he used a sample of only 17 industries), focused on industries where the four-firm concentration ratio was over 60%. He limited his sample in this way explicitly in order to overcome the U-shaped results displayed in column 2 of table 4.1. Stigler commenced his article by accepting, for purposes of testing, 'the hypothesis that oligopolists wish to collude to maximise joint profits'. Thus Stigler's study was not overtly concerned with non-oligopoly or diffuse market structures. Stigler found some relationship between profit rates and four-firm concentration ratios in excess of 80%. But 'there is no relationship between profitability and concentration if . . . the share of the four largest firms is less than about 80%'. This study used 1953—57 data.

Mann's study[5] used 1950—60 data and produced results similar to Bain's. His 21 industries with eight-firm concentration ratios of over 70% showed an average accounting return of 13.3% and his nine industries of below the 70% concentration level a return of 9% — a 4.3% differential, identical to Bain's grouped differential shown in table 4.1.

Weiss[6] cites a further 23 similar studies which had been published by 1969. The majority of these seemed to reveal a weak but nonetheless positive relationship between the two variables. Weiss concludes that 'practically all observers are now convinced that there is something to the traditional hypothesis . . . I doubt that we need many more general concentration-profits studies'.

(b) BROZEN AND DEMSETZ

Two papers by Brozen and one by Demsetz, have, however,

cast doubt on the empirical relationship between concentration and profit rates. No one explicitly addressed the question of the persistence of high profit rates over time until Brozen in 1970.[7] Brozen argued that if there is successful explicit or implicit collusion in concentrated industries then the above-average profits flowing from the collusion should persist over time, other things being equal. The above-average profits would represent a non-competitive equilibrium. On the other hand, if Bain's findings represented a disequilibrium situation Brozen suggested that profit rates in above-average return industries (whether concentrated or not) would decline and those in below-average return industries would rise. (Industry entry would occur due to the attraction of above-average profits. Capacity growth and supply increases would result in relative price falls, and rates of return would converge on the average. Conversely, capacity would contract and rates of return rise in below-average return industries.) Most of the industries in the sample performed in a manner suggesting that they had initially been in a disequilibrium situation. This is illustrated in table 4.2 and holds true for two of the three above-average return industries with low concentration ratios as well as for nine of the 12 above-average return concentrated industries. The 4.3% gap in rate of return between the two groups of industries fell to a statistically insignificant 1.1%.

Brozen carried out a similar exercise on Stigler's sample of 17 industries. Stigler's time period was 1953–57. Brozen replicated the study in 1962–66. Stigler's significant (albeit weak) correlation coefficient fell to a trivial and non-significant level. Of the seven highly concentrated industries (out of eight) which had above-average profit rates in the earlier period, rates of return fell in six. The below-average profitability in the remaining concentrated industry rose.

Brozen also replicated the Mann study. He did this for the 19 concentrated industries for which data were available and which Mann had subdivided by entry barrier height. Mann agreed with and cited Bain in his article to

Table 4.2 Average of industry average-profit rates within concentration deciles, 1936—40, 1953—57, 42 and 98 industries

Concentration ratio (1935)	42 Industry Sample No. of industries	Profitability 1936—40	Profitability 1953—57
90—100%	8	12.7	11.3
80—89.9	10	9.8	11.3
70—79.9	3	16.3	13.8
60—69.9	5	5.8	8.9
50—59.9	4	5.8	12.0
40—49.9	3	8.6	12.5
30—39.9	5	6.3	9.3
20—29.9	2	10.4	10.9
10—19.9	1	17.0	11.7
0—9.9	1	9.1	11.7
0—100	42	9.6	11.1
70—100	21	11.8	11.7
0—70	21	7.5	10.6
Difference		4.3	1.1

Concentration ratio (1935)	98 Industry Sample No. of industries	Profitability 1936—40
90—100%	14	10.0
80—89.9	14	9.7
70—79.9	10	11.9
60—69.9	11	8.2
50—59.9	6	14.8
40—49.9	10	9.5
30—39.9	16	10.4
20—29.9	9	12.0
10—19.9	5	13.4
0—9.9	3	7.6
0—100	98	10.5
70—100	38	10.4
0—70	60	10.6
Difference		−0.2

Source: Table 4.1 and Brozen [7, 11]

the effect that '. . . seller concentration alone is not an adequate indicator of the probable incidence of . . . monopolistic output restriction'.[8] Both Bain and Mann consequently suggest that high entry barriers are necessary along with high concentration to permit monopolistic pricing behaviour in an industry. They therefore classified their highly concentrated sample industries into three groups according to their (arbitrary) judgment regarding height of entry barriers. Table 4.3 shows the effect of recalculating Mann's study at a later date.

Even when only the 'high barriers' group is examined Brozen found that the rate of return fell over time, as it did with the Stigler and Bain unclassified samples. Out of the seven (of eight) above-average return industries in that group, five suffered profitability declines.

Brozen's findings proved unexpected and puzzling to many economists. In particular, he faced the challenge that he had examined industries which were concentrated during the period of the original studies, but which had ceased to be concentrated during the period of his replications. To the extent that this was true, then Brozen argued, there is little cause for concern since, if the market concentration doctrine does hold true at any point in time, then market forces will themselves deconcentrate the industries and reduce the monopoly profits flowing from collusive behaviour.

MacAvoy, McKie and Preston[9] in their response to Brozen adopted the former view. They argued that only industries which had records of persistently high concentration levels should be examined. If this was done then persistently high rates of return would indeed be found. These authors helpfully provided a list of such industries. On examining the specified industries Brozen found that their rates of return were not even high (significantly above average), much less persistently so.[10]

Table 4.3 Movement of average rates of return on net worth for 19 concentrated industries selected by Mann, 1950—60, 1960—66

	1950—60	1961—66
8 Industries with Very High Barriers	16.1%	13.1%
7 Industries with Substantial Barriers	11.3%	8.9%
4 Industries with Moderate to Low Barriers	12.7%	10.0%
Mean	13.6%	10.4%

Source: Brozen.[7]

There remains the original problem of why Bain's original sample showed a significant difference in rates of return in very concentrated industries in one given period. Why should all concentrated industries simultaneously be in disequilibrium? Brozen resolved the problem by showing that there was no correlation that needed explaining. Bain, it will be recalled, examined 42 industries out of 340. Brozen[11] was able to repeat Bain's study using data unavailable when Bain did his original work. Table 4.2 summarises Bain's and Brozen's studies for the same 1936—40 period. With an enlarged and so possibly more representative sample of 98 industries, Brozen's results show that less concentrated industries are the more profitable (albeit insignificantly) by 0.2%. Brozen argues that Mann's and Stigler's small samples were probably similarly non-representative.

While Brozen was arguing for a sceptical attitude towards broad-brush studies of the relationship between concentration and profits, Demsetz[12] was approaching the problem from another position. The earlier studies linked monopoly power and concentration by postulating that fewness in the number of firms in the industry facilitates collusion to restrict output and raise price. Demsetz argued that there are reasons other than collusion for expecting a positive correlation between concentration and profitability. An association between market concentration and rates of return should be expected from any workable incentive system that rewards superior performance.

Superior ability in lowering cost or in improving products, be it the consequence of luck, entrepreneurial or managerial foresight or the presence of scale economies, may well increase profits and draw sales from the unsuccessful towards the successful and efficient firms. Thus concentration and profitability could be associated for reasons totally unconnected with collusion and contrived scarcity. Such situations may be (and Brozen's work suggests they are) eroded with the passage of time as new entrants or existing competitors emulate or improve upon the activities of the successful firm. But unless the short-term monopoly rewards are non-trivial in both amount and duration there will be no incentive for firms to strive towards the performance which produces them.

These sources of profit and market share are specific to the firms which perform well in terms of productive efficiency or innovation. Other firms in the same industry will not share in the higher profits from such sources. But, Demsetz argues, if the only source of higher profits is collusion, then higher profits should be enjoyed by all firms in the colluding industry. The issue then becomes one of ascertaining from which source the profits in concentrated industries arise.

This can be done by examining the correlation between concentration and rates of return for those firms which are relatively small in their respective industries. Since collusion presumably benefits all firms in the industry while superior efficiency benefits only those who can more readily attract custom, this reduces the likelihood of confusing the cause of any observed higher profitability. Table 4.4 details some of Demsetz's results.

It fails to reveal the beneficial effects to small firms which an association of collusion with concentration would suggest. Smaller firms in concentrated industries

Table 4.4 Rates of return by asset size and sales concentration ratios, 1963

Four-firm concentration ratios	No. of industries	Average return	Asset size ($)			
			0.5m	0.5m to 5m	5m to 50m	over 50m
10–20%	14	8.8%	7.3%	9.9%	10.6%	8.0%
20–30	22	8.4	4.4	8.6	9.9	10.6
30–40	24	8.8	5.1	9.0	9.4	11.7
40–50	21	8.7	4.8	9.5	11.2	9.4
50–60	11	8.4	0.9	9.6	10.8	12.2
Over 60	3	11.3	5.0	8.6	10.3	21.6

Source: Demsetz.[12]

are not more profitable than smaller firms in other industries, which is what would be expected if they could shelter under the collusive umbrella of larger firms. The rate of return in the three smallest asset size groupings does not increase with concentration. On the contrary, the data suggest that larger firms in concentrated industries perform at a lower cost than their competitors. In those industries of over 50% concentration ratios, the largest sized firms produce at below average cost. Since a larger fraction of industry output is produced by larger firms in such industries, these concentrated industries should (and do) display higher rates of return than other industries. This is consistent with the many other studies which used data on concentration and profitability from the early 1960s, but it 'may be attributed to the superior performance of the larger firms and not to collusive practices'.[12]

In summary, earlier studies found a small but significant correlation between market concentration and industry profit rates, but these results have not been confirmed by recent work. Any relationship which exists seems to be weaker and less stable than earlier studies suggested. If a subset of industries is examined the relation does not persist more than a few years. The implication of the hypothesis is that concentration facilitates collusion. If so then smaller firms operating in concentrated industries should earn more than smaller firms elsewhere. No correlation between the profitability of small firms and concentration ratios has been found. The fact that large-firm profitability is apparently associated with concentration (table 4.4) might be part of the source of the positive relationship between industry profits and concentration. In the earlier work cited by Weiss[6] industry profits tended to be calculated by averaging the profits of only the large firms in the industries. The divergence between large and small firm profit rates which increases as concentration increases suggests that it is the relative competitiveness of the large firms which is rising as concentration increases, not their monopolistic power.

(c) MEANS AND WEISS

The other major reason why economists began to associate market concentration and monopoly power was the administered price doctrine. This originated in work published by Gardner Means in 1935[13] and 1939.[14] Means examined month by month price changes in US Government price index numbers for selected industries between 1926 and 1933. Some prices changed frequently and others infrequently or not at all over the entire study period. Means used the phrase 'administered prices' to describe those where changes were rare. Such prices were administered by firms rather than being determined by the market by changing cost and demand conditions. Means then divided this sample of industries (a mere 37 of all the then available 282 census manufacturing industries) into more and less concentrated groupings and established that rigid prices were more likely in the concentrated subgroup and that prices tended to decline rather than remain stable in the less concentrated subgroup.

In the inflation of the 1950s Means[15] argued that administered prices in concentrated industries were the primary contributing factor. The obverse of the depression situation held. Prices proved more likely to rise in the concentrated than in the unconcentrated subgroupings of industries. The data Means used in this study were again index data taken from selling-company submissions to the census compilers and matched against the now 30 year old industry classification.

A more comprehensive study of DePodwin and Seldon[16] using a much larger sample of industries appeared to contradict Means' interpretation of the 1953–59 inflation. They found no significant association between concentration and price change. Weiss[17] modified their study, however, and by including variables to take account of changes in demand and cost and their impact on price in 81 industries did discover a greater tendency for prices to rise more in concentrated industries (other things being equal).

(d) STIGLER AND WEISS

At first Means' evidence lacked a conceptual base. This was apparently provided by Sweezy in his article on the kinked demand curve.[18] The paradox that administered prices are said to be rigid in depression conditions and highly mobile upwards in times of inflation can be resolved if one assumes that the kink is then reversed. (The relevant demand curve changes from DPd_1 to dPD_1 in diagram 4.1.)

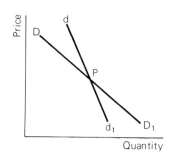

Diagram 4.1

Stigler[19] argued strongly against the logical validity of the kinked demand curve and simultaneously provided evidence that oligopoly prices (from 1929–37) were much less rigid than monopoly prices. (If the theory of kinked demand is correct, then monopoly prices should vary with each fluctuation in cost and demand, provided the monopolist is profit maximising, while in oligopoly they will not, within a certain range, so vary.) Table 4.5 details some of Stigler's results.

However, Stigler's sample is small, and it may be that his monopolies would have had rigid prices (due to cost and demand conditions) irrespective of their structure. Stigler's data, moreover, while contrary to the implications of kinked demand are not necessarily contrary to a general inverse relationship between market concentration and price flexibility.

More recently Stigler and Kindahl[20] removed the

Table 4.5 Price changes in oligopolies and monopolies

	No. of firms in industry	No. of monthly price changes	Coefficient of variation of prices
Oligopolies			
Bananas	2	46	16
Grain Binders	2	5	3
Ploughs	6	25	6
Tyres	8	36	9
Monopolies			
Aluminium	1	2	6
Nickel	1	0	0

Source: Stigler.[19]

empirical foundations from Mean's work. They carried out a survey of transactions prices actually paid by buyers in 70 commodity groups. They sampled an average of 17 customers per group, compared with the normal 2–3 suppliers per group which the official US census takers use as a basis for constructing the Wholesale Price Index. Transactions prices did not behave in the way suggested by the official indices. The indices did not accurately portray the actual behaviour of prices. Table 4.6 details some of the comparisons obtained between the list price index movements and the price paid index alterations.

Even the list price indices are not particularly cordial to the Means' thesis of price rigidity in times of contraction. The transaction prices emphatically contradict it. Similarly, in times of expansion a substantial number of prices move against the predicted direction of the 'administered inflation' hypothesis (nearly half do not move, or decline). Moreover, the sample of industries chosen by Stigler and Kindahl is biased towards highly concentrated, staple commodity type products such as steel, basic chemicals, drugs, paper and petroleum products which have figured prominently in the discussion of 'administered prices'. If anything, the results indicate a tendency of prices to move in the general direction of business, a result which simple price theory would predict.

Table 4.6 Price changes by index number changes in periods of economic contraction and expansion

Contraction periods	List prices	Transaction prices
July 57 — April 58 and May 60 — Feb 61		
Decreases	23	40
No Change (−0.5% to +0.5% per month)	19	10
Increases	26	18
Expansion periods		
April 58 — May 60 Feb. 61 — Nov. 66		
Increases	36	37
No Change	20	14
Decreases	14	19

Source: Stigler and Kindahl.[20]

Weiss[21] repeated his 1953—59 study using 1959—63 data. It will be recalled that in his earlier study he had discovered a positive correlation between concentration and upward price changes, other things being equal. He found no correlation in the later examination, and in yet another repetition of his work (for the period 1963—68) he obtained a negative (but insignificant) association.

One explanation for Weiss' interesting and contradictory results is that in his earlier study industries were readjusting their prices from an abnormally low base which had occurred as a consequence of the price controls imposed during the Korean War. Since it is easier for governments to police price controls in concentrated industries it would be just such industries which had the greatest post-war adjustment to make. Later periods would be unaffected by this phenomenon. Thus it would seem that there is no persistent relationship between inflation and market concentration.

In Europe, Phlips tested for such a correlation using data for countries belonging to the EEC. He discovered also that the relationship between price change and market concentration was either negative or insignificant.[22]

(e) APPRAISAL

The alleged harmful effects of high levels of concentration (monopoly profits, administered inflation and rigid prices) are consequently not proven. To the extent that the thesis does have validity it is *collusion not concentration* which results in prices departing non-optimally from marginal costs. After a period of some three decades when the work of Means and Bain appeared to have stimulated the opposite belief, recent reappraisal of the evidence has tended to encourage a renaissance of the thinking of an older generation of economists. For example, J.B. Clark[23] seems to have been of the opinion that even with only a few firms in an industry, price competition would persist and collusion would be difficult provided that potential competition was a realistic force. The threat of entry, he argued, was as effective in producing the same competitive result as a larger number of firms or the non-colluding behaviour of a few:

> Let any combination of producers raise the prices beyond a certain limit, and it will encounter difficulty. The new mills that will spring into existence will break down prices; and the fear of these new mills, without their actual coming, is often enough to keep prices from rising to an extortionate height. The mill that has never been built is already a power in the market: for it will surely be built under certain conditions. The effect of this certainty is to keep prices down.

Thus profits (and prices presumably unequal to marginal costs) may be transiently associated with industrial concentration. But the two phenomena may not be causally related but rather be simultaneously brought about by successful exploitation of market opportunities such as the attainment of low costs due to scale economies, or the ability to charge a price premium due to the provision of a better product upon which consumers place higher valuations. In short, where there is freedom of entry any gains which firms receive and which are viewed *ex post* as monopoly profits are, from an *ex ante* stance, simply an inducement to creative entrepreneurship.

The empirical facts, therefore, (although mainly

American in origin, and restricted to studies carried out in the last decade) do not support the view that the concentration doctrine is a theory with a good prediction record. Nor does their interpretation suggest that perfect competition is a desirable goal. A static equilibrium with no increased productivity and no product innovations (even if price everywhere equalled marginal cost and monopoly profits did not exist, even for brief periods) is not a state of the world which would appeal to many individuals, workers or consumers.

Earlier empirical work, however, did not support these inferences. But the earlier studies have now been shown to be defective in both research design and interpretation. Unfortunately, the persistently consistent results these studies provided falsely strengthened and added credibility to an unsatisfactory economic theory. How conventional theory has attempted to meet these defects in its predictive value will be discussed in the next chapter. The developments will be shown to be satisfactory until the *importance* of entry is again stressed. That topic in turn leads directly into the Austrian view of competition as a process not a state — a view which will be elaborated on in Chapter 6.

REFERENCES

1   J.S. Bain, 'Relation of profit rate to industry concentration: American manufacturing 1936—1940.' *Quarterly Journal of Economics* 1951.

2   US Congress, Subcommittee on Monopoly of the Senate Select Committee on Small Business, *Role of the Giant Corporations*, Washington 1969, p. 873.

3   Monopolies Commission, *Parallel Pricing*, Cmnd. 5330, HMSO 1973.

4   G.J. Stigler, 'A theory of oligopoly,' *Journal of Political Economy* 1964.

5   H.M. Mann, 'Seller concentration, barriers to entry and rates of return in thirty industries, 1950—1960.' *Review of Economics and Statistics* 1966.

6   L.W. Weiss, 'Quantitative studies of industrial organisation' in M.D. Intriligator (ed.) *Frontiers of Quantitative Economics*, North Holland 1971.

7   Y. Brozen, 'The antitrust task force deconcentration recommendation,' *Journal of Law and Economics* 1970.

8   J.S. Bain, *Barriers to New Competition*, Harvard University Press 1956, p. 201.

9   P.W. MacAvoy, J.W. McKie and L. Preston, 'High and stable concentration levels, profitability, and public policy : a response, *Journal of Law and Economics* 1971.

10 Y. Brozen, 'The persistence of high rates of return in high stable concentration industries,' *Journal of Law and Economics* 1971.

11 Y. Brozen, 'Concentration and profits : does concentration matter?' *Antitrust Bulletin* 1974.

12 H. Demsetz, 'Industrial structure, market rivalry and public policy,' *Journal of Law and Economics* 1973.

13 G. Means, *Industrial Prices and their Relative Inflexibility*, Senate Document, No. 13, 1935.

14 G. Means, *The Structure of the American Economy*, National Resources Committee, US Government Printing Office 1939.

15 G. Means, *Hearings on Administered Prices*, Parts I, IX and X, US Government Printing Office 1957 and 1959.

16 H.J. DePodwin and R.T. Seldon, 'Business pricing policies and inflation', *Journal of Political Economy* 1963.

17 L.W. Weiss, 'Business pricing policies and inflation reconsidered,' *Journal of Political Economy* 1966.

18 P. Sweezy, 'Demand under conditions of oligopoly', *Journal of Political Economy* 1939.

19 G.J. Stigler, 'The kinky oligopoly demand curve and rigid prices.' *Journal of Political Economy* 1947.

20 G.J. Stigler and J.K. Kindahl, *The Behaviour of Industrial Prices*, National Bureau of Economic Research 1970.

21 L.W. Weiss, *The 1970 Midyear Review of the State of the Economy*, Hearings before the Joint Economic Committee, US Congress 1970.

22 L. Phlips, 'Business pricing policies and inflation — some evidence from EEC, *Journal of Industrial Economics* 1969.

23 J.B. Clark, *The Control of Trusts*, 1901.

Effective competition is still dependent on the power of the most competitively minded minority to set a . . . pace that the others are constrained to follow . . . (this) is better than the impossible abstraction of 'perfect competition', largely because of its dynamic quality; and because (of) . . . an increasing role for potential competition.

J.M. Clark
Competition as a Dynamic Process, 1961.

5

Developments in the Traditional Theory

This chapter shows that conventional theory has developed to take account of some of the omissions highlighted in earlier chapters. In particular the importance of entry as a determinant of how far above marginal cost a non-perfectly competitive firm can set its price is now stressed.* Nonetheless the purpose of entry theory, as will be seen, is to investigate why and where a particular equilibrium (or entry-deterring) price will be achieved. The focus of attention is still on competition as a state not as a process. The purpose of the theory is to indicate how much mono-poly profit (due to $P > MC$) a firm can make under given circumstances; it is not to predict how and why firms will initiate changes in supply or react to changes in demand.†

---

* Contrast this view with that epitomised by the quotation from J. Bain at the beginning of Chapter 3.

† For simplicity the methodology of comparative statics is being ignored here. That methodology, however, is more concerned with comparing equilibria than examining the path of adjust-ments. In dynamic analysis the path of adjustment itself is studied. But the reasons any particular path is chosen or deviated from are not. This latter theme will be developed in Chapter 6.

The desirability of (perfect) competition apparently lies in the equivalence of price and marginal cost in equilibrium. Such an equilibrium can theoretically occur in an industry with a multiplicity of sellers. Or it can occur in conditions of natural monopoly where the firm, having reaped all the available scale economies, is subject to suitable regulatory controls. Normal theory regards it as impossible in conditions of profit maximising monopoly, monopolistic competition or oligopoly. Conventional theory goes one stage further. It is argued, as we have seen, that collusive agreements are easier to enter into and maintain when firm numbers are low. In consequence, industrial regulators are advised to pay particular attention to the profits earned by the activity, as well as the high market shares of the colluders. Although this view has now been empirically undermined it is worth restating the plausibility of the arguments which underlie it.

Monopolistic competition is a special, and rare, case. There, monopoly profits are zero, although price is above marginal cost. As in perfect competition profits are zero because of free entry and the number of sellers. In a market of many sellers each is too small for his pricing and output decisions to affect market price. He can sell all he can produce at the market price and nothing above it. He can shade price without fear of retaliation because the resulting output expansion will divert an imperceptible amount of business from each rival. For example, in a market of 100 sellers of equal size, an expansion in output of 20% by one will result in a fall of output of only 0.2% for each of the others. A seller will not worry about rivals' reactions in such conditions.

In contrast, where sellers are few, a price reduction that produces a substantial expansion in the output of one will result in so substantial a contraction of the others that they will quickly respond to the reduction. Say there are three sellers of equal size in the market. Then a 20% expansion in the output of one will cause the output of the others to fall not by 0.2% but by 10%, a contraction the victims are hardly likely to overlook. Thus an oligopolist will be loath to initiate a price reduction *vis à vis* a firm in an atomistic market. He will anticipate a prompt reaction by his rivals which will nullify his gains. Oligopolists are thus interdependent in their pricing behaviour with a consequent tendency to avoid price rivalry.

(a) NUMBERS OF FIRMS

This view that numbers influence firm interdependence, and so price, has a history stretching back to Cournot in the mid-19th century. Cournot argued from two assumptions. First, firms attempt to profit maximise. Second, each firm believes that his rival will maintain a constant output. If these assumptions hold then Cournot's reasoning can be used to support the structure/conduct/performance paradigm. His basic conclusions with regard to numbers are given in table 5.1. A one-firm industry produces the expected 50% of competitive output* and an industry with a very large number of firms produces at the perfectly competitive level. Price, in turn, will be inversely related to quantity produced, and given the same marginal cost levels for each case the departure of price from marginal cost will be greatest when numbers are fewest. Cournot's theory is proved as follows.

Table 5.1

Number of firms in industry	Percentage of perfectly competitive output these firms will produce
1	50.0
2	66.66
3	75.0
4	80.0
5	83.33
6	85.71
7	87.5
⋮	⋮
∞	100.0

* Given a linear industry demand curve, and a horizontal MC curve, marginal revenue will bisect that part of the MC curve to the left of the demand curve.

Consider a duopoly with zero production costs and an industry demand function of

$$P = 100 - Q$$

where $Q = q_1 + q_2$ (the outputs of the two firms). Then if firm 1 regards q_2 as constant, firm 1's demand curve is

$$d_1 = P = (100 - q_2) - q_1$$

and so total revenue is

$$TR = Pq_1 = (100 - q_2)q_1 - q_1^2$$

and marginal revenue

$$dTR/dq_1 = 100 - q_2 - 2q_1$$

Set $MC = 0 = MR$ in order to find firm 1's profit maximising output level. Then

$$100 - q_2 - 2q_1 = 0 \tag{1}$$

If (given and assumed constant) q_2 is awarded values of 10, 20 or $33\frac{1}{3}$ then it can be calculated from equation (1) that firm 1 would choose to produce 45, 40 and $33\frac{1}{3}$ respectively. But firm 2 is operating under identical assumptions and also behaving in a profit maximising manner in the belief that firm 1 will maintain a constant output. Firm 2 will consequently also have a marginal revenue curve similar to equation (1) and so, for any given value of q_1, firm 2's output choice could be calculated. The decisions of the two firms will belie the assumptions each makes about the other, and as each opts for a new output level the other will again choose a new profit maximising level. A mutually consistent equilibrium solution is only attained when

$$q_1 = q_2 = 33.33$$

This assertion can be verified from equation (1). Award q_2 a value of 33.33. Firm 1 will choose to produce an identical amount. Likewise, since firm 2's marginal revenue function is

$$dTR_2/dq_2 = 100 - q_1 - 2q_2$$

then, if q_1 is also awarded a value of 33.33, firm 2 will opt to produce 33.33. Both firms will then be profit maximising and the Cournot assumptions will be fulfilled.

Cournot developed this argument and evolved the general formula

$$Q_n = nQ_c/(n + 1) \tag{2}$$

where Q_c = perfectly competitive industry output and n = the number of firms in the industry. From this formula table 5.1 was computed.

The validity of equation (2) can be proved as follows. Consider a situation with n firms, where $n = 4$. To find the Cournot equilibrium output level for any one firm, assume zero marginal costs and construct a demand curve DD as in diagram 5.1. Divide OD into $n + 1$ (i.e. five) equal parts. Draw FG = OE and parallel to it. Divide FG into n (i.e. four) equal parts. Join BH and project back to the price axis. LB is then any one *firm's* demand curve and LA the relevent marginal revenue curve. LB and DD are parallel so fulfilling the Cournot assumption that the other three $(n - 1)$ firms will hold output constant. Each firm will produce 20% of Q_c, OA for any one firm, OE in total, representing 80% of Q_c where $P = MC$.

But note that quite apart from the restrictive Cournot assumptions, table 5.1 is not really very helpful to the industrial economist. After two or three firms, numbers cease to be significantly important as a predictor of firm output. Since most industries which economists and policy makers analyse in reality, even if far removed from perfect competition, have upwards of three or four firms, this renders the data in the table largely redundant.

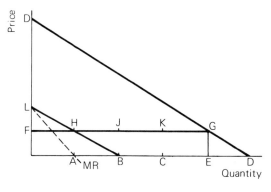

Diagram 5.1

(b) THE IRRELEVANCE OF NUMBERS

It would seem from the above and from the structure/conduct/performance paradigm that price policies of firms depend, at least up to a point, upon the number of firms in a market. They do not. Rather, they depend upon the belief about the policy of rivals attributed to individual firms. Certain assumptions were made in the preceding pages about rivals' reactions. The interdependence assumption in particular seemed to depend on numbers, but there is no essential reason why it should have.

Given the number of firms in a market, a different behavioural outcome will result depending upon the assumption made by an individual firm concerning the reaction of other firms in that group to its own price or output decisions. Or, alternatively, given a belief about rivals' policies, the behaviour of the firm will be the same whether its rivals are one or many.

These propositions were, if not first, certainly most elegantly expounded by G.C. Archibald.[1] We will draw on his paper in the following paragraphs. Consider an industry consisting of two firms producing an identical product. If each firm assumes (Cournot style) that its competitor will maintain its output irrespective of the price it charges then each firm will consider it faces a demand curve such as d_F in diagram 5.2 where D_I is market demand. d_F is parallel to D_I given the assumption that the rival firm is

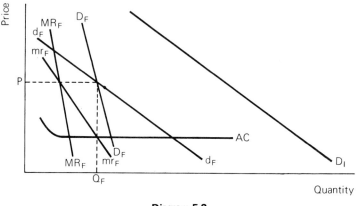

Diagram 5.2

expected to maintain a constant output (and so match any price cuts or price increases made by the firm under observation).

To profit maximise given these assumptions the firm will equate mr_F with marginal cost and produce Q_F at price P. But if each firm acts in the same way and has the same assumptions, the d_F curve of the diagram is simply the 'particular' or dd' curve of Chamberlinian analysis. It 'slides down' the 'share-of-the-market' demand curve D_F, (or DD' in Chamberlinian terms). The firm will continue to set a price on a curve such as d_F, which will continuously result in an output short of expectations until an equilibrium level such as that in the diagram is reached, where both the actual and the expected marginal revenue curves cut the marginal cost curve. As long as d_F, the expected or particular demand curve, is higher than its equilibrium position, then mr_F will also be above MC. Price will consequently be lowered and output increased in order to maximise (expected) profits.

If we maintain the assumption that each firm continues to believe that its rival will maintain a constant output in the face of price changes, then increases in the number of firms do not change this analysis. With two firms in the industry and a random distribution of custom, $D_F = \frac{1}{2} D_I$. With three firms D_F is shifted to the left to equal $\frac{1}{3} D_I$ and so on. Ultimately, depending on cost conditions, the

Chamberlinian tangency solution of zero monopoly profits
will be arrived at. The tangency solution, however, is
dependent not on the number of firms, but on the assumptions each makes about the others' behaviour, and on the
particular cost conditions ruling in the given industry.
Thus in diagram 5.1, it would have been a simple and
theoretically correct task to construct the figure so that the
cost curve, AC, and the imaginary demand curve, d_F, were
tangential to each other.

What *does* take place when firm numbers are increased
is that the price elasticity of demand rises for each firm,
whether measured on D_F or d_F. This is not surprising given
that in perfect competition price elasticity is infinite. But
it may appear too much to swallow when it is recollected
that the slope of D_F becomes progressively steeper as
numbers rise and D_F pivots in towards the vertical axis;
and that d_F retains the same slope as D_I and is merely
shifted bodily downwards to the left as numbers rise.

The explanation of this apparent paradox is simply that
elasticity (η) is the product of the reciprocal of slope and
the ratio of price to quantity, and this can be moved
towards infinity as easily by altering the price:quantity
ratio as by altering slope. For example, if D_I can be represented by the function

$$p = a - mq$$

where m is slope and a is the intercept with the quantity
axis, then d_F can be represented thus:

$$p = a - m(q_1 + q_2)$$

where $q_1 + q_2 = q$. Then:

$$p = a - mq_1 - mq_2$$

Since q_2 is assumed constant this can be rewritten:

$$p = k - mq_1$$

Clearly it is irrelevant what number of firms contribute output to k, and slope $= m$ whatever the size of k. Thus the horizontal demand curve of perfect competition is not realised by varying the number of firms. Elasticity, however, in the limit will approach infinity.

The elasticity of the market demand curve D_I, is:

$$\eta = \frac{p}{q} \frac{1}{m} = \frac{p}{qm}$$

$$= \frac{a - mq}{qm} \tag{3}$$

and that of the particular demand curve, d_F

$$\eta_F = \frac{a - mq}{q_F m}$$

If firm F's share of the market is $S_F = q_f/q$ then

$$\eta_F \cdot S_F = \frac{a - mq}{q_F m} \cdot \frac{q_F}{q}$$

$$= \frac{a - mq}{mq} = \eta \ \text{(from equation (3))}$$

Thus

$$\eta_F = \eta/S_F$$

But as the number of firms rises, F's share, that is S_F, approaches zero and so η_F approaches the infinity of perfect competition; but the demand curve does not become horizontal, and price does not come to be equated with marginal cost.

To obtain the horizontal demand curve of perfect competition it is necessary to change the firm's assumption about the policy of its rivals. Instead of the assumption that competitors strive to keep output constant (by price matching) the assumption must be made that each and every firm believes that changes in its output do not alter price. For example, *if firms believe that rivals will not change price* in response to their actions, then the particular demand curve, d_F, for an individual firm at a price slightly below that of its competitors will be horizontal up to the total quantity demanded by the market at that price. Attempts to undercut each other's prices will then *result in an equilibrium price of P = MC for individual firms, totally irrespective of numbers.*

Alternatively, if each assumes that others will imitate both its price and its output strategy then the equilibrium industry price and output combination will be (assuming constant and equal marginal costs for each firm) the same as would result under conditions of monopoly. In other words, the industry would be operating under idealised cartel-like conditions.

(c) THE IMPRACTICALITY OF CARTELS

A cartel is an agreement among independent firms to act in accord with regard to their market decisions. They take decisions with the welfare of the group as a whole in mind rather than engaging in rivalrous behaviour. In this way they hope that their *pro rata* shares of joint monopoly profit will be greater than the individual profits they could make if they did not act in accord.

Diagram 5.3 illustrates the basic principles underlying cartel pricing. In panel (b) D_I represents the industry demand curve. S is the market supply curve, obtained by aggregating horizontally the MC curves of the numerous independent sellers in the industry. Without collusion the market price would be P_1 and the quantity produced and sold would be Q_1 where $P = MC$. Any single seller would produce and sell Q_4 units, where $Q_4 = Q_1/n$ where n = the number of (equal sized) firms in the market. If any single seller were to sell an additional unit his marginal revenue would be insignificantly different from P_1. For the group as a whole, however, MR would be significantly

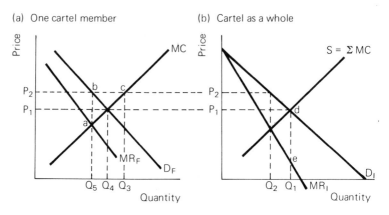

(Quantity axes drawn on different scales.)

Diagram 5.3

below market price. (Geometrically this is obscured in the diagram since the quantity axis in panel (a) is a 'stretched out' version of the same axis in the second.)

If the sellers collude as a single monopoly the profit maximising price—output combination is $P_2 Q_2$ where $MC = MR_I$. As long as all firms have identical MC curves P_2 is also the optimum price for the individual cartel member. Since we are assuming that all sellers act in concert, when one reduces quantity there will be a perceptible effect on price. If a single seller acted alone his demand curve would be almost horizontal at P_1, but since what any one does they all do, D_F, the 'share-of-the-market' curve is the relevant demand curve.

Had the two panels in the diagram been drawn on the same (quantity) scale the distance $(Q_1 - Q_2)$ would be n times as great as $(Q_4 - Q_5)$. Given concerted action the profit maximising output for the single firm is Q_5 at the cartel price P_2 where $MC = MR_F$. With joint profit maximisation made possible under collusion, why do cartels invariably break down?

There are three main reasons: the 'free rider' problem; varying marginal costs; and the fact that rivalry has many other dimensions than price.

Each colluder is expected only to supply Q_5. This is a

quota which somehow the cartel must enforce. But each firm realizes that if he alone supplies more than Q_5 the effect on price will be negligible. P_2 is the price each firm must take. If a firm acts alone P_2 is his marginal revenue curve. The quantity that then maximises profit (under these changed assumptions and given that others continue to price at P_2) is Q_3. The individual seller makes a profit gain of *abc*. Since this opportunity is open to all the probability is very high that one or a few firms will seize it. A cartel may be a 'gentleman's agreement' but, as Stigler pithily pointed out, 'the participants seldom are, or long do'.[2] Each firm will be tempted to gain a 'free-ride' on the anti-competitive behaviour of his fellows. Since profits attract entrepreneurs like honey attracts bees then, unless a sufficiently powerful overseeing body can enforce the output quotas and/or inhibit new entry, the cartel will inevitably crumble. Generally only a state or government agency has such far-reaching inquisitorial powers of inspection and enforcement.

Two good examples of cartels are IATA (the International Air Transport Association) and OPEC (the Organisation of Petroleum Exporting Countries). IATA could only keep North Atlantic air fares high for as long as entry by firms such as Laker Airways was prevented. The airlines themselves could not prevent Laker's entry but the UK and US governments, or their regulatory agencies could, and did. Eventually the governmental bans were withdrawn. Laker entered, fixed its fares at a low price and was promptly closely matched by existing carriers.

OPEC, on the other hand, has no super-governmental body to appeal to for aid. Oil prices fell in real terms despite the existence of OPEC until the Arab-Israeli war of 1973 (OPEC was formed in 1960). In 1973 the FOB sale price of Saudi Arabian oil rose from $2.12 to $7.61 per barrel, of which 60 cents went to the oil companies, and $7.00 to the Saudi government. By 1975 the Saudi take had risen to $10.12, the companies' take had fallen to 38 cents, and the price was $10.50. Most other sellers matched this price schedule. In 1974 oil consumption fell by several percentage points in most of the important buying countries. This reversed the trend of rising demand which had persisted in the consuming countries for most years since World War II. 'Free-riding' was rife. In 1974 OPEC production of crude fell by 1.3%, but the two leading producers, Saudi Arabia and Kuwait had cut production by 8.4% and 35.7% respectively in that period. Without a supranational body to curb entry or free-riding the OPEC cartel could only hold prices high if individual members were prepared to carry the 'free-riders' by drastically cutting their own production and revenues. Our theory suggests this cannot persist in the long run.*

In diagram 5.3 we assumed that each firm's MC curve was in the same position so that equal quotas resulted in equal marginal costs. Suppose, however, that marginal costs vary. Assume as in diagram 5.4 that there are only two sellers and that the collusive agreement is that each will supply half the quantity demanded at each price. D_F is consequently the 'share-of-the-market' demand curve for each firm and the MR curve for the group as a whole. MR_F is each firm's perceived marginal revenue curve and MC_A and MC_B are the MC curves for firms A and B.

The optimum prices for A and B are thus different, namely P_A and P_B. They will disagree over which price should be set for the group. Moreover, the cartel's optimum price, P_C, is not the optimum for either of the two firms. Cartel profits are maximised, not when the quantity to be produced is necessarily divided equally, but rather when $MR_I = \Sigma\ MC$. This occurs when output is divided so that $MC_A = MC_B$ in order that each firm might have the same marginal cost. (If $MC_A \neq MC_B$ at *any* output level, then output reallocation should take place between the two firms until the marginal equivalency condition again holds. Without such reallocation the cartel would not be minimising costs and so would not, even if operating at the profit maximising output level, be maximising the difference between revenue and costs.) Thus, if an output of

---

* This example is discussed more fully in J. Hirshleifer, *Price Theory and Applications*, Prentice-Hall 1976.

Q_1 and a price P_C could be agreed upon, the cartel would face formidable difficulties in allocating output in the profit maximising manner. Firm A would wish to produce more than Q_A and B less than Q_B. Again only an agency with strong powers of coercion could ensure that the cartel would not disintegrate. Again this is likely only if some government body exercises industrial oversight.

The final reason why cartels tend to collapse is that if the cartel, with or without government enforcement, successfully establishes a 'floor' price then rivalry is likely to break out in dimensions other than price. Product-related services will become more lush, advertising will rise to stress the benefits of such extras and the cost curves of each firm will rise. Under conditions of open competition profits are eliminated by price rivalry. In the case of a successful cartel they may be eliminated by an increase in cost, e.g. airlines, with the backing of the International Air Transport Association, maintain centralised prices and compete by providing more leg-room, more cabin attendants, better meals, more frequent flights, larger or otherwise more attractive aeroplanes than the market requires. As G.L. Bach[3] put it, in another context, such an arrangement might not be 'a halfway point between competition and monopoly, but rather an arrangement that combines the worst characteristics of each and the benefits of neither'.

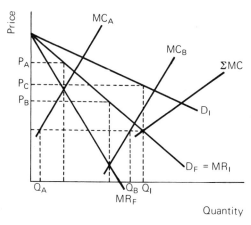

Diagram 5.4

Output is not at minimum average cost, price is not equated with marginal cost, scale economies may not be achieved, and average cost curves may be higher than need be. If there is freedom of entry to the cartel then, if the cartel is otherwise operating 'successfully', these problems may be compounded.

(d) THE MEANING AND IMPORTANCE OF ENTRY BARRIERS

Contrary to the last statement, absence of entry barriers is generally and correctly regarded as a means whereby competition is facilitated and its benefits obtained. (In the cartel conditions cited it merely further increased industry operating costs and generated still further excess capacity.) In normal circumstances, however, markets must have freedom of entry and exit to operate efficiently in allocating resources away from low valued uses towards high valued uses.

Although free entry has a long history as an integral part of the theories of both perfect and monopolistic competition[4] it is rarely if ever introduced automatically into discussion on the theory of oligopoly. In fact, several theories of oligopoly ignore entry. Early discussions of oligopoly (e.g. Cournot) varied the numbers of firms but did not attribute the variation to entry. The increase in numbers was simply given, not explained. Later, more complex models where each seller assumes that his rivals will not remain inert but will react to any given marketing initiative provided richer insights than Cournot type models. But they embraced variations in the conjectures of each firm regarding rivals' reactions (and variations in the accuracy of and response to these conjectures) rather than entry.

Game theory, one variant of these approaches, also fails to eliminate indeterminacy in complex cases, and it too ignores entry. Other theories examine oligopoly from the stance of cartels and again largely ignore entry. For example, Fellner, devoted a whole book (*Competition Among the*

Few, 1949) to the problem. But Fellner's approach to the topic is to regard oligopoly as being a group of non-collusive firms with joint profit maximisation as a goal. What facilitates attainment of this goal and what barriers there may be to its attainment are examined (e.g. profit division disputes, uncertainties and errors, risk aversion and preference, product differentiation, coordination of innovation, pricing and output and so on). Fellner's oligopoly, in short, differs from a pure cartel only in degree.

Fellner approaches the problem qualitatively and entry had little part to play in his discussion. Stigler, more recently, attempted to quantify the probability of cartel instability.[5] He studied the reasons why collusion is unlikely to persist, which we have already examined (particularly the 'free-rider' problem from price-shading) and suggested situations in which such conditions were more or less likely. Again entry was largely ignored.

Stigler, however, was one of the first to pinpoint the importance of entry to oligopoly theory. Commenting[6] on Fellner's book he noted that all oligopoly theories as they stood (in 1950) must be non-rational and inconsistent. This must be so since (a) the theories attempted to explain the behaviour of firms assuming that they seek to maximise their individual profits, (b) monopolisation was the only conceptual solution but (c) such collusion was assumed incomplete or costly to achieve. He argued

> perhaps we should change our line of attack. One alternative formulation (rather than asking how A and B treat each other) is: why do firms A and B constitute the industry and how long will they enjoy this position? That is, what are the conditions of entry of new firms and expansion of existing firms in an industry? ... when attention is turned to this question, oligopoly behaviour loses much of its arbitrariness and oligopoly price much of its indeterminacy ... This formulation ... reduces (the oligopoly problem) to a minor aspect of a more manageable problem.

Stigler was largely correct and by the end of that decade Joe Bain,[7] Sylos-Labini and Franco Modigliani[8] had all produced work which now forms a synthesised and widely accepted theory of entry in oligopoly conditions.

The theory of entry barriers rests on one principal

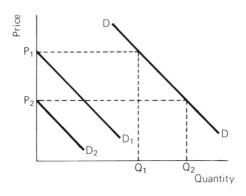

Diagram 5.5

assumption known as the Sylos postulate. This alleges that
potential entrants expect established firms to maintain
their output levels (i.e. to reduce price to accommodate
the entrant) in the face of entry, and that this expectation
is, in the event of entry, actually fulfilled. Diagram 5.5
illustrates how a potential entrant can calculate where his
demand will lie if he is considering entering a given industry.
DD is the demand curve for the industry. Existing firms
are producing Q_1 units of output at price P_1. Given the
Sylos postulate an entrant must increase the industry's
total output and therefore the industry's price must fall
by a sufficient amount to clear both Q_1 and the additional
output of the entrant. Effectively, therefore, the entrant's
demand curve is that segment of the total industry demand
curve to the right of the ruling price. This will be $P_1 D_1$ if
the ruling price is P_1, or $P_2 D_2$ had the ruling price–output
combination been $P_2 Q_2$. To ascertain whether or not to
enter an industry a potential entrant will compare this
perceived demand curve with his particular perceived cost
function.

Entry barriers are of three main types: product differentiation or consumer preference barriers, absolute cost
advantages, and scale economies. Analytically, the former
two can be grouped together. Preference barriers and
absolute cost barriers are present if established firms have
lower average unit costs than potential entrants at any
given output level. Thus, to overcome preference barriers,

entrants might have to spend more highly on advertising or research and development than existing firms. To overcome absolute cost barriers they may have to pay higher input prices than established firms, as, for example, when an established firm controls a scarce input such as a patent right or a raw material source from which royalties or discriminatory prices can be extracted. Scale economy barriers exist when there is a declining LRAC for the product in question which makes it difficult for a smaller firm to enter the market given its substantially higher costs or, alternatively, precludes entry by a large firm if the market is of a given size, and any unsatisfied demand can only be met by a small firm.

Where such entry barriers exist, 'under the Sylos postulate, there is a well defined maximum premium that oligopolists can command over the competitive price' (Modigliani). The lower are the entry barriers, the closer is the price to the (perfectly) competitive level.

This is illustrated in diagrams 5.6 and 5.7. In diagram 5.6 absolute cost barriers exist. The entrant's average total cost curve, ATC_E, is higher than that of established firms, ATC_F. Established firms can produce at a price:output combination of P_1Q_1 and the demand curve confronting the entrant is consequently P_1D_1. At no point on that curve can an entrant possibly make a positive profit. Had established firms been selling at price P_2, output Q_2, the

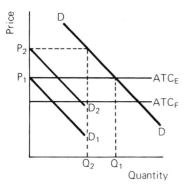

Diagram 5.6

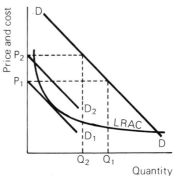

Diagram 5.7

entrant's demand curve would have been P_2D_2 and entry would have occurred, pushing price down once more to the entry-deterring level. The height of the entry barrier is measured by the difference between the entry-deterring price and the ATC_F curve. This difference is in turn dependent on the difference between the two ATC curves.

In diagram 5.7 the LRAC curve for all firms in the industry is displaying scale economies. The entry-deterring price:output combination is P_1Q_1. The demand curve P_1D_1 facing a potential entrant at no time allows him to make a positive profit. Again, had established firms been producing at price P_2, output Q_2, then the entrant's demand curve would have been P_2D_2 and a substantial range of output over which profits could be made would have induced entry, pushing price down again to the entry-deterring or limit price. The height of the entry barrier is measured by the vertical difference between P_1 and the LRAC curve at output Q_1. The practical effectiveness of this barrier is dependent upon a combination of factors including the price elasticity of demand, the scale at which the LRAC levels off or begins to rise, and the size of the market itself.

This view of barriers to entry has not gone unchallenged. The line of attack has been twofold. First, it has been asserted that the tripartite division of entry barriers into absolute cost advantages, product differentiation and scale economies is misleading, because scale economies are *not* and product differentiation *need not be* barriers. Second, there are *other* important barriers to new competition which are not embraced by or included in Bain's triumvirate.

Stigler[9] defines a barrier to entry 'as a cost of producing (at some or every rate of output) which must be borne by a firm which seeks to enter an industry but is not borne by firms already in the industry'. This definition would be readily accepted by most if not all economists. But after a careful examination of the definition it will be seen that indeed scale economies are not and product differentiation need not be impediments to the entry of new firms into an industry.

Consider economies of scale. The strength of these as a barrier is often measured by either of two yardsticks. These are the minimum efficient scale (m.e.s.), of output (where the LRAC curve becomes virtually horizontal) expressed as a percentage of the relevant market; and the percentage increase in unit costs if a firm operates at some fraction (usually half) of the m.e.s. The former indicates the maximum number of firms which could operate at full capacity in the industry; the latter indicates the cost penalty incurred by smaller firms. Thus in diagram 5.8 in industries A and B m.e.s. equals one third of industry demand at a price equal to minimum LRAC. Three firms could thus operate at full capacity in these industries and earn normal profits. However, in industry A the steep rise in LRAC at scales less than m.e.s. indicate that a firm operating at sub-optimal scale would incur a high cost penalty, thus virtually precluding entry. This compares with industry B where a small-scale firm would incur a relatively small unit cost penalty and hence small-scale entry would be more feasible. Other things equal, it is then reasonable to assume that industry B is easier to enter profitably than industry A. In industry C, where m.e.s. is achieved at just over 8% of industry demand, 12 firms

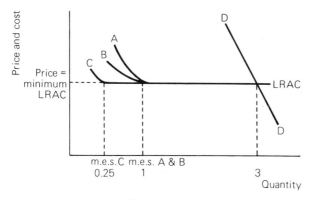

Diagram 5.8

could operate at full capacity and the scale barrier would be minimal.

But Stigler[9] argues that '(it) would be equally possible to say that inadequate demand is a barrier to entry, (since if) we define a barrier as a differentially higher cost of new firms, there is no barrier . . .' In fact a logical consequence from Stigler's point, made by Brozen[10] is that the long-run equilibrium amount of capacity in a perfectly competitive industry is also an entry barrier. No firm with standard technology would be tempted to enter such an industry any more than it would be tempted to enter one where scale economies and limited demand have resulted in only a single firm occupying the market with a price equal to the average cost required to supply the market at that price. New firms under either of these conditions do not face a differentially higher cost. Rather, what economies of scale do (along with demand) is determine the *size* of firms which will exist in an industry.

Similarly, product differentiation is only an entry barrier if the costs of differentiation are higher for new than for existing firms. Early empirical studies of advertising as an entry barrier explicitly used a model where this was the case. Comanor and Wilson alleged that existing firms 'need not incur penetration costs.'[11] Their theory was based on a diagram similar to 5.9 which shows a range of long run average cost curves. Economies of scale in both advertising and manufacturing are assumed. Curve A is the unit cost curve for advertising and promotion required to maintain any given sales volume once it has been established and given the general market demand. Since only the entrant requires to incur market penetration costs, that is only he requires to spend high initial levels of advertising monies in order to bring his new product to the market's notice in the face of existing brand loyalties, it is then a truism that his ATC curve, S, must exceed the ATC curve of existing firms, T, at each and every output level. In the absence of scale economies the barrier to entry would be represented by P_0, while with the addition of scale economies in both advertising and manufacturing, plus an

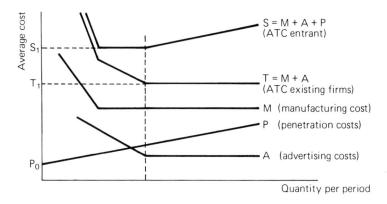

Diagram 5.9

assumed increasing cost of attracting ever more loyal customers from existing firms, the barrier would rise to $S_1 - T_1$ compared with a firm of optimum size. P, average penetration expenditure at each output level for the period relevant to the diagram, is obtained in the same way as any other cost curve would be derived from known capital expenditure. The period can be assumed to be one year and P can be expressed in annual equivalent form by multiplying the required capital outlay by the cost of capital and dividing the result by the number of units sold. This is a mis-specification of theory, however. Annuitised penetration costs are incurred (by definition) annually. Thus curve P should be included in both S and T. It is then less apparent that advertising (or product differentiation expenditure) is an entry barrier. If advertising is an entry barrier then any study which attempts to ascertain whether advertising and (monopoly) profits are associated must be wary in its use of data. Comanor and Wilson[11] as would be expected from the discussion to this point, did not adjust the accounting data they used to embrace the fact that advertising creates an intangible asset. To do so it is necessary to redefine the profits—capital ratio by increasing the denominator to include advertising as an asset, and to alter the numerator by deducting 'advertising depreciation' costs and adding back that part of current advertising expenditure which is, in fact, asset creating.

Comanor and Wilson's original results that profitability is greastest in those industries where advertising:sales ratios are highest is then open to question. In a repetition of their study[12] where they corrected for these effects Comanor and Wilson again obtained similar results. Other writers, for example Bloch,[13] have rejected a relationship between advertising and profitability.

However, for the purpose of our discussion, the direction of such empirical evidence. is unimportant. The original thesis was that the relationship would exist because profits were shielded by high entry barriers. There is little theoretical support for this proposition. To the extent that the relationship exists it may well be due to other factors (e.g. advertising can be associated with innovation, or with an attempt by entrepreneurs to mitigate risk; profits may then arise from innovation and risk, not from advertising).

To the extent that product differentiation is indeed an entry barrier, that is it imposes differentially higher costs on new firms, it must be because they have to incur higher penetration costs than do existing firms. *A priori*, arguments can be produced which would plausibly support either this view or its obverse. A new entrant can more easily insinuate itself into a market if its product is not identical to existing offerings. Buyers, after all, are unlikely to switch to a new supplier unless its product more efficiently serves their tastes than those already available. Markets may be more competitive, more open to entry with product differentiation than without it. Buyers dissatisfied with a product from a current supplier will more readily search for an alternative source of supply if there are no barriers to the offering of alternative varieties.

On this view, barriers to product differentiation can be the impediment to entry, not product differentiation itself. So the argument comes full circle. What are barriers to product differentiation and how can they be imposed? The answer is similar to that in our discussion of cartels. Only collusion can inhibit product differentiation. Only government support, tacit or overt, can maintain or coerce a long-lived collusion by producers. Only government has the power to impose legal restraints on entry based on product differentiation. (For example: the spread of supermarkets in the UK until the abolition of resale price maintenance in 1964 was inhibited by the difficulty of making the self-service variant of their product attractive through the medium of lower prices — only those customers who preferred self-service irrespective of price, patronised the supermarket; the long fight which Laker Airways had with government bodies on both sides of the Atlantic to be allowed to introduce its 'no-frills' 'Skytrain' London-New York air service; the dramatic decline in product innovation in pharmaceuticals following the 1962 amendments to the Food and Drug Act, in the USA, a decline which was six times as great as that experienced in the UK where similar testing regulations were *not* introduced, and which resulted in the British market receiving the benefits of major pharmaceutical innovations four to five years ahead of the USA with consequential benefits for competition and the consumer, in this case the sick).

Before concluding this section it is worth examining the case of 'natural monopoly'. A natural monopoly is a firm which is the sole seller and producer of a good whose technology makes single firm production cheaper than any other alternative. Here we have a basic dilemma. Free entry may encourage cost control and stimulate innovation, but a given market size may only accommodate one producer at least cost. Are the competitive benefits of entry and those of scale economies and least cost production dichotomously opposed? Is this not a case where industry must be either government regulated or owned to prevent monopolistic practices by the producer? Demsetz[14] has answered these questions in the negative.

Demsetz bases his case on the argument that there is no necessary relationship between the number of *producers* as determined by demand and cost conditions on the one hand, and the number of *bidders* for the market's custom on the other. Competition is always *for* the market not *in* the market. This distinction, however, is generally overlooked. Even in a multiproducer market producers compete for custom against each other; they do so in the context of the market for that good but that is not a necessary condition. Demsetz says 'the determinants of competition in market negotiations differ from and should not be confused with the determinants of the number of firms from which production will issue after contractual negotiations have been completed.'

For example, the plant and equipment in a natural monopoly may be in government ownership (e.g. the oil fields of the North Sea or Mexican Gulf, or the television airwaves and the transmitting equipment in the UK). Open market bidding could then take place periodically for the right to use that plant and equipment (in the case of the oil fields this is done on a once-for-all basis, in the case of the TV networks the Independent Broadcasting Authority does it at intervals of approximately ten years). That is, there could be competition for the right to service a market for a specified period of time whenever there could not be competition in the actual sale of services themselves. (The TV example, it is worth noting, is *not* in fact a natural monopoly, there could be competition in that market.) Many rival entrepreneurs could be in on the bidding for the right to service a given area. Each bidder would have to guarantee a fixed return to the owner of the plant to cover depreciation and interest costs. The winning bid would be the one that offered the lowest price to consumers over the life of the contract (as in the case, say, of telephone rates and charges) or provided the government, as owner on behalf of the community, with the highest income (so passing back any monopoly profits to society) in those industries where the product is provided at zero price to consumers. The difficulty with the latter procedure is how to devise a low cost mechanism which will pass back the monopoly profits to the relevant members of society from whom they were first abstracted (but more sophisticated methods of metering consumption, such as pay TV, may enable the winning bidder to charge consumers, thus restricting the government's role simply to that of selecting the lowest bid). This optimistically assumes the government will not establish anti-competitive tendering rules for political reasons.

Finally, freedom of resource movement also implies freedom of industry exit as well as of entry. Bankruptcy, takeover and mergers are the devices used in the market place to shift resources from a less-valued to a more-valued use. Again only government can prevent these devices being employed. Unfortunately, government's record as an alternative director of resources is poor. In Britain, for example, the nationalisation and 'lame-duck' policies of successive governments have become notorious as examples of how productive resources can become immobilised in industries producing goods for which there no longer is a consumer demand, e.g. the steel, shipbuilding, motor car and motor cycle industries.

(e) COMPETITION AS A PROCESS

Entry then, when correctly defined, is a prerequisite of competition. Actual entry or threat of entry, is or can be present in all forms of market structure through to natural monopoly. Given open entry into bidding for markets, firms cannot control supply and price and make a market monopolistic in terms of a deliberately imposed and long maintained inequality of price and marginal cost. Entry, however, does not always occur when $P > MC$. And $P > MC$ is a situation which may persist, or a gap which may widen, even in the presence of entry. Why is this so? Are some entry barriers insurmountable?

Exclusive access to a given raw material or resource may shield a firm from entry. But such a barrier is likely to be of only short-term duration because alternative sources of the input will be discovered or changing technology will make possible the use of alternative raw materials. If the superior resource is the entrepreneur himself, and his skills are scarce then the firm will make above-normal profits and the entrepreneur will collect rent on his superior skills. Even this is likely to be only a short-run barrier to entry. Superior entrepreneurs do not necessarily breed children or train colleagues who will also become entrepreneurs of supranormal ability.

It is sometimes said that if it takes a vast sum of money (financial capital) to set up shop in an industry then entry is effectively impeded. One of the functions of the capital market is to provide entrepreneurs with start-up funds. If an entrepreneur can convince others that he can successfully enter a market then he can obtain funds by borrowing or by selling ownership rights. Since information is not free, however, not all potentially successful entrepreneurs will be able to convince others of their ability. (Only a crystal ball could do that.) As a consequence, the financial market will provide funds to some who, *ex post,* are failures, and not to others who, *ex post,* might well have been successful. This indicates that the capital market is imperfect and so a possible barrier to entry. It must be emphasised, however, that this 'imperfection' exists only because information is not free. This is as meaningful a statement as bewailing that man was evicted from Eden.

The whole story of entry implies mobility. Resources move from one (low-valued) use to another (higher-valued) use. The entrepreneur is the individual who reallocates the resources. Why does he do so? He does so because he, and he alone, perceives an opportunity to capture profits as a result of the cost and demand conditions which he perceives will exist on that future day when he concludes his transactions. The entrepreneur must be alert to profit opportunities on an *ex ante* basis. As Ludwig von Mises put it, the market tends to eliminate from the entrepreneurial role all except those able 'to anticipate better than other people the future demand of the consumers'.[15]

In Chapter 1 we viewed profit as a reward for a kind of arbitrage. But that arbitrage is very different from the simplest case where price differentials exist in different markets simultaneously for the same product and are known to all. Entrepreneurial arbitrage arises when the prices of resources in factor markets today (costs) are not in full adjustment with the prices of final products at their date of sale (tomorrow). The entrepreneur notices the discrepancy before others do. What distinguishes it from simple arbitrage is not the different nature of the goods (inputs and final products), since the bundle of inputs contains all that is necessary to obtain the final output, but rather that input purchases precede sales. Product prices do not yet exist except as anticipations. 'What makes profit emerge is the fact that the entrepreneur, who judges the future prices of the product more correctly than other people do, buys some or all of the factors of production at prices which, seen from the point of view of the future state of the market are too low.'[16]

It will now be evident that competition as a process, if it is to ensure that price does not persistently exceed marginal cost requires entry. But it will also be apparent that entry need not occur in all cases where $P > MC$, and this lack of entry need not be due to either the presence of entry barriers or even a capital market with lack of full information. Any observed excess of price over marginal cost can be viewed, *ex post,* as monopoly profit. But if entry is free then the profits from the *ex ante* view are simply the inducements to creative entrepreneurial innovation.

Entry can rarely occur instantaneously, and the entrepreneur reaping these *ex ante* rewards may simply be in the situation of the firm in diagram 5.10. Time lags must generally exist before entry can occur. If a time lag does

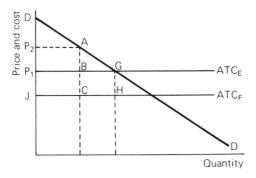

Diagram 5.10

exist, for example to enable the entrant to erect and tool up a new factory, then it may be worthwhile for existing firms to price above the entry-deterring level to obtain the benefit of a short-run profit maximising price. Diagram 5.10 illustrates the nature of the calculation which will be made. Assume the existence of absolute cost barriers to entry and assume also a zero discount rate. It will pay the existing firms to charge the short-run profit maximising $(MR = MC)$ price of P_2, rather than the entry deterring price of P_1 if in so doing the profits for the period before entry plus the profits for the period after entry are greater than the profits which could be earned at P_1 for the total period to which the industry demand curve applies. Thus P_2 will be charged initially (and P_1, of necessity, after entry) if, in algebraic terms, P_2ACJ (for the period before entry) + P_1BCJ (for the period after entry) is greater than P_1GHJ (for the total period).

The entrepreneur on this Misesian view is carrying out a form of arbitrage and is consequently helping narrow the price spread. Goods are being supplied in the final product market at a lower price or at an earlier date than otherwise would have been the case. Resources from the factor markets are being awarded a higher price, closer to their valuation by society (as society views their values today from the standpoint of tomorrow) than they would otherwise have received. Entrepreneurship raises the present values of both consumers' and producers' surplus. It moves the market closer to a situation of price = marginal cost.

As a digression it is worth comparing this notion of entrepreneurship — ever moving the market towards equilibrium — with Schumpeterian entrepreneurship. Schumpeter saw the entrepreneur as an innovator who did 'new things'. He shifted the cost or revenue curves which faced him and reaped profits accordingly. He is, to quote Schumpeter, a 'disequilibrating' element.[17] A Misesian entrepreneur, on the other hand, does not shift these curves, but is the first to notice 'that they have in fact shifted'.[18] He then acts to restore equilibrium by engaging in the arbitrage process we have described.

This narrows the price spread and provides him with profit. This in turn brings the profit opportunities to the attention of less alert entrepreneurs who in their turn enter the market and further narrow the gap between price and marginal cost. Thus entrepreneurial activity is always competitive. The only possible barrier to an alert entrepreneur exploiting a perceived opportunity is access to resources. Thus we have come full circle. Of Bain's triumvirate of entry barriers we cast doubts on the correctness of including scale economies and product differentiation, and accepted only absolute cost disadvantages (due to resource owners either refusing to sell to others at the price of the resource to themselves or being unable to sell to others due to indivisibility or to legal impediments).

Schumpeter's view that the innovator's profits must be protected by some form of entry barrier from the Perennial Gale of Creative Destruction for a sufficiently long period to provide 'the baits that lure capital on to untried trails' may seem to contradict our approach. In one sense it does. If Schumpeter is interpreted as asking for barriers to entry as a means of encouraging entrepreneurship which will shift the economy from a level of equilibrium to a higher but disequilibrium level, then this is antagonistic to the Misesian view. (It is, however, relatively faithful to Schumpeter's own theorising.) But if Schumpeter is merely seen as asking that entry be slow enough (not barred altogether) so that the innovator can earn more by innovating than by not innovating then we can reconcile, but not equate, Misesian and Schumpeterian entrepreneurship. The Misesian entrepreneur will already have taken into account in his estimate of future cost and demand conditions the probable length of his estimated 'head start' and the impact on his net revenue of successive entry by later entrepreneurs. In short, if resources are not monopolised (or government regulated) then the Misesian entrepreneur will be only too well aware that he has no monopoly of entrepreneurship and so no possibility of perpetually reaping *ex post* monopoly returns.

The next chapter develops the role of the entrepreneur

in Austrian economic theory. Chapter 7 then attempts to answer the question: who in fact are those entrepreneurs in the capitalism of the last quarter of the twentieth century?

REFERENCES

1 G.C. Archibald, ' " Large" and "small" numbers in the theory of the firm', *Manchester School of Economics and Social Studies* 1959.
2 G.J. Stigler, *The Theory of Price*, Macmillan 1966.
3 G.L. Bach, *Economics*, Prentice-Hall 1968, p. 364.
4 M. Blaug, *Economic Theory in Retrospect*, Heinnemann 1968, pp. 381–3, 402.
5 G.J. Stigler, 'A theory of oligopoly', *Journal of Political Economy* 1964.
6 G.J. Stigler, 'Capitalism and monopolistic competition – a discussion', *American Economic Review* 1950.
7 J.S. Bain, *Barriers to New Competition*, Harvard University Press 1956.
8 F. Modigliani, 'New developments on the oligopoly front', *Journal of Political Economy* 1958.
9 G.J. Stigler, *The Organisation of Industry*, Irwin 1968, p. 67.
10 Y. Brozen, 'Competition, efficiency and antitrust', *Journal of World Trade Law* 1969.
11 W.S. Comanor and T. Wilson, 'Advertising, market structure and performance', *Review of Economics and Statistics* 1967.
12 W.S. Comanor and T. Wilson, *Advertising and Market Power*, Harvard University Press 1974.
13 H. Bloch, 'Advertising and profitability: a reappraisal', *Journal of Political Economy* 1974.
14 H. Demsetz, 'Why regulate utilities?', *Journal of Law and Economics* 1968.
15 L. von Mises, *Human Action*, Hodge, 1948, p. 288.
16 L. von Mises (1948), pp. 253–4.
17 J. Schumpeter, *Capitalism, Socialism and Democracy*, Harper and Row 1948, p. 132.
18 I. Kirzener, *Competition and Entrepreneurship*, University of Chicago Press 1974, p. 81.

(Entrepreneurs) are the first to understand that there is a discrepancy between what is done and what could be done.

Ludwig von Mises, *Human Action,* 1963

6

Competition, Entrepreneurship and Exchange

In this chapter the role of the entrepreneur will be examined in more detail. Entrepreneurs compete with each other to satisfy consumer wants. The more rapidly and accurately an entrepreneur anticipates consumer wants and the more successful he is in forecasting how these wants can be satisfied at a low cost to himself the more profit he makes. In order to realise a profit (or a loss if he is unsuccessful) he must arrange a trade between the consumer and suppliers of relevant factor inputs. This chapter will examine in turn the basic principles of trade and exchange, the entrepreneur and competitive equilibrium.

(a) TRADE AND EXCHANGE

Ever since Adam Smith wrote about the 'invisible hand' and the propensity of men to 'truck, barter and exchange' trade has been one of the central topics of economic analysis. Trade and exchange, in the sense Smith studied them, were spontaneous, unplanned activities guided only by the 'invisible hand' of self-interest. In his book, *Human Action,* von Mises defined this study of the exchange process as 'catallactics'.

Catallactics is derived from the Greek 'katallatein' meaning 'to exchange', 'to make an enemy into a friend'. The word is a good one since no voluntary trade will be entered into unless *both* parties feel that they will be better off as a consequence. A catallaxy is the spontaneously produced market order where these exchanges take place. It arises because of the working of the 'invisible hand'. By definition, such a market does not have its objectives known in advance, and it cannot therefore be organised in a pre-designed manner from above.

Unlike a centrally planned society (or Robinson Crusoe on his island) production and consumption decisions are not predetermined. Nor can Lord Robbins' logic of choice be applied. The optimal allocation of known scarce resources to serve prescribed purposes implies knowledge and agreement in advance. The 'invisible hand', the 'catallaxy', works by competition. Competition between entrepreneurs is the mechanism used for discovering desired purposes that are not foreknown.

Before examining entrepreneurial competition, the way in which trade can 'make an enemy into a friend' will be examined. How is trade a beneficial activity?

One way to explain this is to use the well-known tool of indifference curve analysis. Indifference curves rest on three main assumptions:

(a)   everyone wants more of many goods;
(b)   there is always some amount of any good which will induce each person to give up some of any other good;
(c)   each person's marginal evaluation of a good will decline the more he has of it.

The first assumption rests on the plausible belief that no one has enough of everything. And to get more of any particular good something else must be given up to obtain it. Few goods are 'free'. Even clean air can only be obtained by either incurring the costs of living and working in a rural area, or incurring commuting costs, or by all city dwellers forgoing in-city transport.

The second assumption follows the first. Provided a person can get sufficient in exchange of a particular good or goods, he will always be prepared to forgo some part of what he already has. The concept of the marginal rate of substitution (MRS) rests on this assumption. The MRS of good X for good Y is the maximum amount of Y a person will give up to get one extra unit of X. It shows how much value the person places on one unit of X, at the margin, in terms of Y. The MRS is a purely subjective phenomenon. It shows the value to the buyer of Y in terms of X. It shows his willingness to pay and is unique to him. It has nothing whatever to do with measures such as the costs of production. It depends solely on individual preference, and shows the strength of individual *wants.* It has nothing to do with what people say they *need.* Need is an irrelevant concept in the analysis of exchange. Wants, on the other hand, are basic to catallactics. They show how much a person is prepared to sacrifice in order to obtain what he wants.

The third assumption asserts that what a person is prepared to give to get an extra unit of a good will decline the more of that good he has. The maximum price, the reservation price an individual will pay for a good will fall the more he has of it.

From these assumptions hypothetical indifference curves can be drawn for any one consumer. Indifference curves connect points of equally desirable combinations of bundles of goods. Say in a two-good (X and Y) world a consumer has an indifference curve as drawn in diagram 6.1. Then from that indifference curve (or isoquant) can be drawn five conclusions. (The axes represent quantities of Y and X respectively.)

1.   At point B, EF is what would willingly be given up by the consumer in order to obtain DG of X (and vice versa). EF:DG is the MRS of X for Y; this follows from assumption (b).

2.   Less of Y must be compensated for by more of X if A is to be as equally desirable a combination

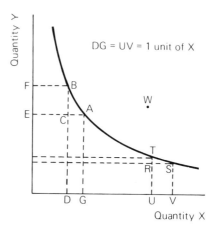

Diagram 6.1

for the consumer as is point B. The curves slope
down from left to right; this follows from assumption (a).

3. As more of X is possessed, its marginal value falls.
    The MRS of X for Y is less on the arc ST than on
    the arc AB. BC:AC > TR:RS. The curve is convex
    to the origin; this follows from assumption (c).

4. Points above an indifference curve are more satis-
    factory than those on it. W is preferred to A, B, S
    or T; this follows from assumption (a).

5. Many isoquants with different values can be drawn.
    Some indifference curve passes through point W;
    this follows from assumption (b).

With this framework it can now be shown that voluntarily negotiated trades are beneficial to both parties to an
exchange. Exchange does not benefit one party at the
expense of another.

Consider two individuals, A and B, in a two-good, Y and
X, world, with indifference curves as shown in diagram 6.2.
Each currently possesses bundles of Y and X as indicated
by the original endowment points E_A and E_B. Their
marginal evaluations of Y and X are not the same. A values
1X at 3Ys (or 1Y at ⅓ X) but B thinks 1X is only worth
1Y (or 1Y is only worth 1X).

Both individuals can be made better off if each acquires some of the good he values more highly from the other. For example, if B gives 1X to A in exchange for 2Ys, B moves to T_B and A to T_A (where T_A and T_B represent transaction or trade points).

B would have been willing to accept anything over 1Y (to induce him to give up an X) and he receives 2Ys. A would have been willing to pay anything under 3Ys (to obtain an X) and he pays 2Ys. Diagram 6.2 does not explicitly imply that points T_B and T_A will be the trades actually negotiated. It does not definitely state what exchange prices will be agreed upon, but the trades will take place in the direction of the arrows, and the price will be somewhere between 1Y and 3Ys for the traded X. Any price (in terms of Y) between these limits will result in both A and B becoming better off (moving to a higher isoquant). As they trade, their marginal evaluations come closer to each other. A's MRS declines from 3:1 of X for Y and B's MRS rises from its original 1:1 ratio. Trading continues until no further mutual gains are possible, that is until their respective MRSs are equal (at 2:1 in this instance).

An alternative geometric device, the Edgeworth Box, can be used to illustrate the same exchange procedure. In diagram 6.3 the indifference curves for A and B have been superimposed after first swivelling B's by 180°. The precise positions of the respective origins O_A and O_B are determined by ensuring that the original endowment

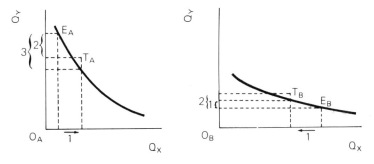

Diagram 6.2

points E_A and E_B coincide at E. In this way the total height of the Edgeworth Box measures the quantity of Ys held in aggregate by A and B, and similarly the breadth is restricted to the limited total of Xs held by the two individuals.

At E, since the indifference curves intersect, their slopes and hence their MRSs and the marginal valuations of X and Y held by A and B differ. The arrows indicate the trading process. When A moves from Y_A to Y'_A and gives up two units of Y, B acquires a corresponding amount. Similarly, A's positive acquisition of 1X from B is exactly counterbalanced by B's movement from X_B to X'_B. T will be a point of mutually beneficial trading and is equivalent to T_A and T_B in diagram 6.2. No more trading will occur since, at this point, both A and B have identical valuations of Y in terms of X. Their respective indifference curves passing through T will be tangential to each other. A's minimum selling price for Y is the same as B's maximum buying price for Y (in terms of X).

In diagram 6.4 a series of possible indifference curves are shown for A and B. Possible trade points are shown at C, D and F. If initial endowments had been at E_1 then the parties would have exchanged and traded to end up between isoquants A_2 and B_2. In fact, they would trade until they

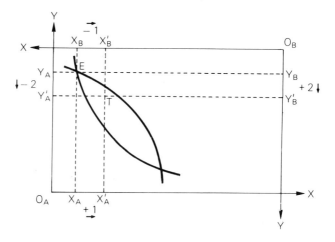

Diagram 6.3

arrived somewhere on segment CD of line GF. This line, GCDF, is the contract curve and is drawn in such a way that it connects all points of tangency between indifference curves, that is all points of equal marginal rates of substitution.

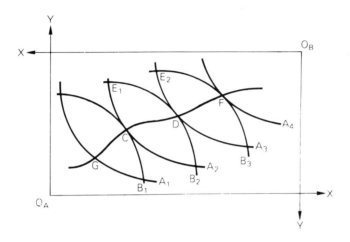

Diagram 6.4

(b) ENTREPRENEURIAL ORIGINS

Entrepreneurs can be regarded as middlemen — albeit very special types of middlemen. Here we will try to conceptualise the entrepreneurial function by looking first at the simplest type of middleman — the middleman who facilitates trading between A and B in the situations detailed in diagrams 6.2–6.4.

In the illustration described above, A and B traded face to face. This is unusual. Normally trade takes place with a middleman. Why? The basic assumption of the earlier illustration was that A and B knew each other and could communicate at zero cost. But transaction costs (e.g. information processing, transport, search by buyer and seller, etc.) are rarely zero.

Buyers and sellers do not normally know each other. They would have to search each other out and find out from each other what mutually beneficial exchange opportunities existed. These search and exchange costs could be diminished if a specialist third party undertook them, and collected information about bids and offers for a fee. Such a specialist could trade between A and B at less expenditure of time and effort than if they had traded directly.

For example, in diagram 6.2 a middleman could offer B 1.5Ys for 1X, which is 0.5Y more than B's minimum supply price. He could take that X to A and offer it to him for 2.5Ys which is 0.5Y below the maximum price A is willing to pay for 1X. The middleman ends up with 1Y and both A and B are better off than they were (they are on higher isoquants). Without the middleman, and with heavy transaction costs (search, transport, bargaining), either the trade would not have taken place or exchange and transaction costs in excess of 1Y might have been incurred.

In diagram 6.4, had the initial endowment point been such that the difference between the MRSs was 0.5Y and, had the cost of engaging in trade, even using a low cost specialist middleman, been 1Y, then trade would not occur. A and B would remain at that endowment point and not move onto line GCDF.

When a middleman spots the possibility to promote a trade between parties who have either previously been unaware that such a possibility exists, or who have been deterred by high transaction costs, then that middleman has spotted an entrepreneurial opportunity. When he promotes that trade he is acting entrepreneurially. When his transaction costs, including any reward for the bearing of risk and any (actual or imputed) interest he must pay to the providers of capital, have been deducted from his income the residual is entrepreneurial profit.

(c) ENTREPRENEURSHIP AND CONVENTIONAL PRICE THEORY

In the conventional theory of price the objective is to define the conditions of optimisation in a given situation.

For example, in terms of diagrams 6.2—6.4, *given* endowments E_A and E_B, *given* the tastes and preferences exemplified by the relevant isoquants for A and B, only definite and precise values of the quantity variables X and Y, and of the price variables (the MRSs), are consistent with an equilibrium situation. The objective of conventional theory is to determine a point on the contract curve; it is *not* to tell us how that point is arrived at. In a search for equality of the marginal rates of substitution we are deflected from the more interesting and relevant tasks of asking why the entrepreneur/middleman arranges the mutually beneficial exchanges; of asking how he is made aware of opportunities for arranging trades; of asking how he informs A and B that trade possibilities exist; of asking how his function can be carried out more efficiently; of asking how he reacts to changes in the given data of endowments, preferences and production possibilities?

In conventional price theory 'efficiency' obtains in equilibrium. In the theory of competition as a process, efficiency does not depend on the equality of price with marginal cost or the equivalence of marginal rates of substitution, 'rather, it depends on the degree of success with which market forces can be relied upon to generate spontaneous corrections ... at times of disequilibrium.'[1]

This process of correction is the function of the entrepreneur. 'Entrepreneur means acting man in regard to the changes occurring in the market.'[2] And when Mises refers to the entrepreneur in this way he is not referring to capitalist or worker, to manager or employee, to producer or consumer. Any of these can be an entrepreneur. 'Economics, in speaking of entrepreneurs, has in view not men, but a definite function.'[3] So by inference any producer, consumer or resource owner who acts in response to change is, to a greater or lesser degree, an entrepreneur.

In equilibrium, therefore, there is no place for the function of entrepreneurship. In equilibrium, or what Mises called an 'evenly rotating economy'[4] there are no changes in the given data of endowments, technologies or preferences. In such an imaginary economy in which all transactions and physical conditions are repeated without change in each cycle of time there is no uncertainty. Everything is imagined to continue exactly as before, including all human ideas and goals. Under such fictitious constant repetitive conditions there can be no net change in any supply or demand and therefore there cannot be any changes in prices (or marginal valuations or marginal contributions). But as soon as these rigid assumptions of given data are abandoned it is clear that action must be affected by every data change. Since action is directed towards influencing the future, even if 'the future' is simply the next instant, then action is affected by every incorrectly anticipated data change between the initiation of the act and the period towards which the act is directed. 'Thus the outcome of action is always uncertain. Action is always speculation.'[5]

This explains how every economic actor is an entrepreneur. There is no such thing as a perfectly predictable action. Moreover, this discussion can help highlight the differences and similarities between the Schumpeterian and Misesian concepts of 'entrepreneurship'.

In a chapter headed 'How the economic system generates evolution' Schumpeter identified innovation as one of the principal promoters of economic change and growth.[6] Innovation was defined by Schumpeter to include not only the introduction of new products and techniques but also the opening up of new markets and supply sources, the improvement of management techniques and new distribution methods. The person responsible for doing these and other 'different things' is the entrepreneur or innovator. The entrepreneur, to Schumpeter, is a factor input and like other factor inputs must be rewarded. It is the payment for entrepreneurial services which forms Schumpeter's well-known concept of profit as a reward for innovation. 'It is the premium put upon a successful innovation in a capitalist society and is temporary by nature; it will vanish in the subsequent process of competition and adaptation.'[7]

Here are highlighted both the differences and the similarities between the Misesian and Schumpeterian entrepreneur. Mises' entrepreneur, like Schumpeter's, acts for anticipated personal gain. But the Misesian entrepreneur is *any* human actor motivated by gain. In diagrams 6.2–6.4 two individuals, A and B, gained from the process of trade. In discussion it was shown that the trade could also have been initiated by a middleman. The spotting of the opportunity for gain, the initiation of the necessary action, and the capturing of the (uncertain) profit are all the functions of an entrepreneur. At some stage of the exchange *each* of A, B and the middleman had to act entrepreneurially. It is possible that each incurred similar entrepreneurial effort and reaped similar rewards, but it is more probable that one of the three assumed the greatest part (but not the whole) of the entrepreneurial role. No one can be wholly passive, no one can take totally predictable actions, no one can opt out of entrepreneurship except in equilibrium.

So both Schumpeter's and Mises' entrepreneurs act in accordance with the 'invisible hand' in order to obtain profit or gain. In this way their notions can be reconciled. But the differences are more important than the similarities. Schumpeter's entrepreneur moves the economy away from one equilibrium towards another higher level equilibrium. Mises' entrepreneur, however, helps move the economy towards equilibrium, but that equilibrium is itself an ever changing and unattainable objective. Schumpeter's entrepreneur can be studied within the context of an evenly rotating economy where particular individual changes are initiated by the innovator and the logical effects of these particular changes deduced via the principles of marginal equivalency. This can be a valid and useful method of analysis but it tells us little of the market process itself.

Before turning to the market process, it is worth emphasising that conventional economic theory has not ignored either entrepreneurs (at least as defined by Schumpeter) or the concept of uncertainty. What it has failed to embrace is the Misesian entrepreneur and the handling of uncertainty in the presence of *changes* in the underlying *(already uncertain)* market conditions.

Conventional theory permits transactors to make once-for-all exchanges at ruling equilibrium prices. It also permits search behaviour whereby in the presence of imperfect information about the optimal equilibrium, time and effort and other costs can be incurred by transactors to find out the terms on which goods are available on the market. After a point, search will be abandoned in favour of waiting or queueing for a commodity or service because the marginal costs of search themselves are about to exceed the marginal benefits of further search.

Alternatively, conventional theory permits transactors to take decisions using a wide variety of techniques developed explicitly to take account of different contingent outcomes.* Moreover, Bayesian decision theory enables transactors not only to take decisions using probability theory (prior analysis) but also enables them to collect further information and revise their probabilistic expectations in the light of information so acquired (posterior analysis).

But as Littlechild points out, none of these elaborations on conventional theory meet the aim of understanding the market process.

> (All of) these models more or less run down as the agents discover all there is to know . . . To see why this should be so, let us look more closely at the assumptions in the models. The agents are equipped with forecasting functions and decision functions to enable them to cope with uncertainty. Indeed the agents *are* these functions. But though their specific forecasts and decisions may change over time in response to changes in economic conditions, the *functions themselves remain the same.* The agents never learn to predict any better as a result of their experiences. Nothing can ever occur for which they are not prepared, nor can they ever initiate anything which is not preordained.'[8] (Emphasis in original.)

Eventually they simply move towards and reach (at least in theory) the questionable Nirvana of equilibrium.

(d) ENTREPRENEURSHIP AND AUSTRIAN ECONOMICS

The epigram which defined the Misesian entrepreneur at

---

* For a discussion of some of these techniques see my *Managerial Economics* Philip Allan 1975, Chapter 1.

the beginning of this chapter can now be seen to be much fuller and richer than it appears at first sight. The entrepreneur (be he producer, consumer, middleman or resource owner) does far more than merely bring together two parties and facilitate a mutually beneficial exchange between them (as in diagrams 6.2–6.4). The entrepreneur is the person who is *alert* to the presence of such opportunities before anyone else perceives them.

The entrepreneur notes, *ex ante*, that the indifference curves of consumers are different tomorrow from what they are today. He notes *ex ante*, that the production isoquants of producers are not the same tomorrow as they are today.

The entrepreneur may make mistakes in his predictions, or he may be correct: in which case he makes losses or profits. The entrepreneur must choose which prediction he believes to be correct. But he cannot simply choose to facilitate a process which equates *current* marginal valuations. Professor Shackle says: 'Decision is choice amongst rival available courses of action. We can choose only what is still unactualised; we can choose only amongst imaginations and figments. Imagined actions . . . can have only imagined consequences.'[9]

Even without changes in basic market data (consumer tastes, production possibilities and resource endowments) decisions made today generate a new series of decisions tomorrow. Today's decisions (the commencement of the market process) are made in ignorance of these basic market data. As the market process unfolds this ignorance is reduced and each market participant revises his bid and offer prices in the light of what has occurred and what he has now learnt about to or from whom he may wish to sell or buy. *The process is inherently competitive* since each successive set of offers and bids is more attractive than the preceding one. That is, every individual offer or bid is being made with the awareness that all others are now being made with fuller knowledge of the advantageous opportunities available. Since that is so, each individual participant knows that he cannot offer less attractive trading opportunities than his competitors. He (and they) must continually inch ahead of his (their) rivals.

Even without changes in basic market data this competitive movement towards equilibrium brought about by entrepreneurs must occur. If it did not, the potential traders would not trade. In terms of diagrams 6.2–6.4, A and B would go to market and return home empty handed. Would-be traders (would-be self-improvers motivated by the invisible hand) would fail to realise that they could exchange unless they (or a middleman) *learn to alter* their bid and offer prices, that is unless someone acts in an entrepreneurial manner. The competitive process is 'analytically inseparable' from entrepreneurship.[10]

Now let us examine changes in the basic market data. If technology and/or tastes change, or if new types or quantities of resources are discovered, then any of the information contained in diagram 6.3 relating to the indifference curves of either A and/or B and/or to the dimensions of the Edgeworth Box itself, and so to the relative position of the endowment point E, will be affected. Market disequilibrium is not then simply a pattern of prices and quantities subject to change under competitive pressure from the entrepreneurial arbitrage function. It is not then simply a case of an actual or hypothetical middleman offering a seller a marginally higher price and a buyer a marginally lower price than would satisfy either, and pocketing the (net of costs) difference as profit. With changes in the basic data this same process is occurring as the 'middleman' offers buyers other marginal improvements (such as a wider product range, or a higher quality product) and/or as he provides sellers with conditions or opportunities for sale not previously on offer.

To accomplish these things the 'middleman' or entrepreneur must generally also incur costs. But his net-of-costs profit does not arise through *him* exchanging something *he* values for something *he* values more. It comes about rather because he has been alert enough to discover sellers and buyers with such different valuations. Pure entrepreneurial profit arises from *'the discovery of something obtainable for nothing at all*.[11] (Emphasis by Kirzener in his original text.)

(e) IMPLEMENTATION OF ENTREPRENEURSHIP

Conceptually entrepreneurial profit is the reward which accrues to that unique someone who is alert enough to take it. The very act of grasping what is already there will alert less wakeful entrepreneurs to do the same so that over time the combination of arbitrage and entry ensures that such profits fall to zero. Such a process will work itself out competitively or begin again when another such opportunity appears and is noticed by the most alert to have emerged.

Of course, the entrepreneur in practice may well have to involve other market participants before he can grasp his profits. He may, but need not, combine the entrepreneurial role with that of one of these other participants. Other market actors include consumers, producers and resource-owners.

An entrepreneurial consumer, as an individual, may seek out improved exchange opportunities. So too might a producer. But it is worth pointing out that both production and consumption can be subsumed under exchange. For example, Robert Clower argues: 'An ongoing exchange economy with specialist traders *is* a production economy since there is no bar to any merchant capitalist acquiring labour services and other resources as a "buyer" and transforming them (repackaging, reprocessing into new forms, etc.) into outputs that are unlike the original inputs and are "sold" accordingly as are commodities that undergo no such transformation. In short, a production unit *is* a particular type of middleman or trading specialist'.

Austrians such as Mises, Hayek and Kirzener would agree with much of Clower's view. But they would disagree with Clower when he says 'that "capitalists" are just individuals who have the wit and forethought to exploit profit opportunities by . . . engaging in the "production" of both trading services and new types of commodities.'[12] Those with the 'forethought' are the entrepreneurs. Capitalists are resource owners who *may* combine that function with that of entrepreneurship.

One needs to look no further than the 19th century history of retail cooperatives in the United Kingdom to see how consumers, too, can perceive entrepreneurial opportunities and exploit them. The fact that the retail cooperatives came to employ resources of land and labour and have accumulated trading capital to purchase other forms of stocks and equipment may mean that some entrepreneurial acts in the modern consumer cooperative are inspired by resource owners such as managers or capitalists but the proximate entrepreneurship was undoubtedly that of consumers.

At the individual level also, consumers seek out favourable exchange opportunities. But in the modern industrial economy the costs of entrepreneurial activity, the costs of generating alertness to the potential of gain, is more generally carried out by resource owners, producers and consumers of intermediate products rather than by consumers of final products. It tends to be *firms* which carry out competitive price adjustments in both a situation of static and of changing market data. Final consumers tend to buy or not to buy according to the valuations they place or will place on the offered commodities.* The more complex the economy, the greater the variety of goods and services available, the more likely this is to be true. The consumer has only a limited time span in which to carry out entrepreneurial search (there are a fixed number of hours in the day). Yet the range of purchase opportunities continues always to increase. It is not surprising, then, that more and more of the entrepreneurial role is being undertaken by producers.

---

* Final consumers are entrepreneurs in that they search for better trade possibilities. But, in general, more effort is incurred by firms placing before consumers an array of such opportunities from which to choose. Firms search out consumers more actively than consumers search out firms.

Not only is the firm (or the entrepreneurial component of the firm) constantly adjusting or being forced to adjust its offered price to bring it closer into line with consumer wants, the firm is also constantly attempting to adjust its whole commodity offering. In the light of changing technologies, resources and consumer tastes, the entrepreneurial component in the firm will not only be attempting to bring bid and offer prices marginally closer together* but will also be attempting to bring the range and quality of apparently and potentially tradeable goods and services closer together.

In this way product differentiation, research and development, selling cost and advertising will all be engaged in by competitive firms attempting better to satisfy consumer demand.

When a producer-entrepreneur incurs costs to satisfy what he perceives *will be* consumer demand, he is doing so to win anticipated revenue in excess of his anticipated costs. He will gain that anticipated profit only if he competes more successfully than others in meeting demand. His costs will include the normally defined manufacturing costs and also the conventionally defined advertising costs. But no 'single penny of the outlay . . . (manufacturing or advertising costs) . . . can be perceived as anything but costs incurred in order to "sell" '.[13]

Diagrams 6.5 and 6.6 use the technique of comparative statics before and after new products have been launched onto the market to illustrate some of these issues. It is assumed that:

(a) The development of new products is a primary objective of many firms. The preferred market position which such new products can provide is the main incentive for this objective.

(b) Firms will expand output to the point where the least profitable unit will be produced at a marginal

---

* Only marginally, in order to capture as much business as possible from higher priced rivals; not totally, otherwise the entrepreneurial profit arising from different marginal valuations will not exist.

cost equal to price. Clemens[14] in his original model stressed the use of idle capacity, but here the movement by firms towards meeting unfulfilled demand for unanticipated wants producing either 'major', 'minor' or even 'insignificant' advances over existing products is emphasised.

(c)   There is a high cross-elasticity of supply between markets in both production and research activities. This permits the demand curves under examination to be considered in commensurate units (in terms of inputs required to produce a heterogeneous range of outputs).

(d)   There is low cross-elasticity of demand between a firm's products, viz. their demand curves tend to relate to different consumer wants.

(e)   The market positions of the firm's various products range from strong market power (e.g. newly patented products) to perfect competition (e.g. multi-source, generic-like commodities).

Diagram 6.5 is the basic, static-situation, Clemens model. It shows five separate demand curves for one firm, with profits maximised where marginal revenue is equated for each and the limit set by the market with the perfectly elastic demand curve. Cocks then used diagram 6.6 for a comparative static analysis of price and product quality competition. He asserts that 'price competition . . . would

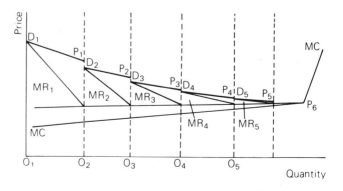

Diagram 6.5

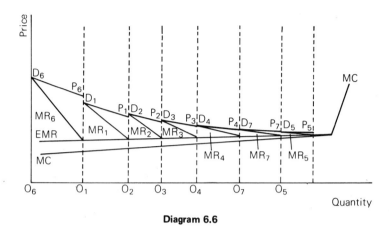

Diagram 6.6

be reflected by a shift of the demand curves D_1 through D_5 downwards and towards greater elasticity'.[15]

Diagram 6.6 depicts the firm shown in diagram 6.5 in a subsequent period when it has successfully introduced a new product significantly better in consumers' eyes than existing products. Demand curve D_6 represents this innovation. While the firm was developing this product, competitors could readily see the profit potential of the product associated with, say, D_5. They had an incentive to enter with products of thir own, and such entry would cause the elasticity of D_5 to become greater. The introduction of the new product, D_6, alerts competitors to the profit potential of the innovation also. At the same time the firm in diagram 6.6 is introducing its significant new product, it could also be entering product areas of competitive firms (D_7) with demand curves like D_5 in diagram 6.5, or any other product area in which price is greater than marginal cost. This increases the elasticity of the demand curves faced by these competitors.

The equilibrium towards which this process moves would embody a price tending towards marginal cost for at least some firms in every market where innovation took place. This is not unlike the tendency to Paretian optimality. If the $P : MC$ ratio on the intra-marginal sales of all firms merely reflects differences in the research and development (R & D) or other innovative costs attributable to producing the relevant new product for the intra-marginal markets, the (hypothetical) outcome would be a very close approximation to perfectly competitive equilibrium. Moreover, even if the $P : MC$ ratio does not do this, i.e. fall, allocative efficiency is still likely if these consumers just on the margin of buying are provided by a firm operating at $P = MC$.*

The outcome of this argument is that industry is not purely competitive in the sense of static micro-theory. Rather, the pricing behaviour of this industry suggests a competitive process with a welfare loss in the static sense but where the 'monopoly rents' implied are actually the sources of funds for the R & D which develops new products in the future. Thus the dynamic element must be considered. These 'rents' represent social-opportunity costs in the sense that they partially represent what society forgoes if prices behave in the manner suggested and not in the manner predicted by the standard theory of perfect competition. Thus in order to obtain innovations in the future, society must forgo certain benefits today represented by product prices being greater than marginal manufacturing costs. This 'welfare loss' is the social marginal cost of R & D, promotion and innovation, so that if this is added to the 'production costs' the total marginal social cost may well come close to being equated with the product price. The pricing outcome in practice would imply that for any individual existing product the innovative or entrepreneurial marginal social cost or 'wage' is transitory as prices are eroded over time, so that for the industry as a whole new products must be introduced on a continuum in order to maintain this marginal social cost in order, in turn, to provide the benefits of trade and entrepreneurship on a continuing basis.

In brief, the static model of perfect competition is an inappropriate tool with which to analyse the economic performance of any entrepreneurial industry. Even when the microeconomic model is extended to embrace oligopoly in a static framework, it still fails to take account of the

---

* For an expanded, but alternative, version of this argument see F.M. Scherer, *Industrial Pricing*, Rand McNally 1970, p.132.

richness and complexity of the real-life variables that determine product price and quality. A theory is required that is both dynamic with respect to price and quality and defines marginal cost sufficiently accurately to embrace entrepreneurial rewards. Only then can meaningful price: marginal cost comparisons be made.

Moreover it may be impossible to ascertain objectively either *ex post* or *ex ante* which of the entrepreneur's costs have resulted in a 'better product' and which have 'changed consumer tastes'. Certainly, changing technologies may result in alert producer-entrepreneurs manufacturing different products. But (final) consumers are rarely in a position to exercise entrepreneurial alertness to exploit such changing technologies, or even to exploit the changing manufactured output possibilities. The producer-entrepreneur in the modern complex economy emerges as an advertiser in order partially to relieve *'the consumer of the necessity to be his own entrepreneur'* (emphasis in Kirzener's original statement).[16]

But advertising also increases the consumer's alertness to the entrepreneurial opportunities which he himself can grasp. It increases his effective range of choice from which to select the option which provides him with the greatest benefit from trade. But selection implies rejection, which implies that he has been alerted to the existence of sources of supply which are offering lower prices *or more satisfactory products* than they need have done in order to induce him to purchase. In short, *advertising can increase the consumer's role as entrepreneur* at the same instant as it decreases it.

Edward Chamberlin did economics a disservice when he used the term 'monopolistic competitor' to describe the producer producing a unique product slightly different from his neighbour. He is no monopolist. So long as freedom of entry exists, so long as the neighbour *can* do exactly what the original firm is doing, the fact that he is not is simply a result of his differing entrepreneurial judgement. Competition involves rivalry in other dimensions than price.

Chamberlin, in *The Theory of Monopolistic Competition,* drew a distinction between 'production' and 'selling' costs.* Yet we have argued above that this is a false dichotomy. If there are two products otherwise similar to the outward eye but which are considered different by the consumer, then to the economist these *are* different products.

Ludwig von Mises gave the example, which is difficult to improve upon, of eating in a restaurant. A man has a choice of two restaurants serving identical meals — but in one the floor has not been swept for six weeks. The food is the same. Is the money spent by one in sweeping the floor 'production costs' or 'selling costs'? Does sweeping change the food? No. Surely, then, it could be argued that this is strictly a 'selling cost.' It is like advertising. The food remains the same: but because the customer has seen a man sweeping the floor, more people come to this restaurant than to that. But this is a fallacy. What one buys in a restaurant is not the food alone, but a meal in certain surroundings. If the surroundings are more desirable the meal is different. The package or image is different. That which is spent to change the total product (including the image) is as much a production cost as the wage paid to the chef. Both alert customers to the price and quality of the product.

The entrepreneurial role, then, can be seen as conceptually distinctive, but in reality it is predominantly (but not exclusively) embodied in the entity known as the firm. The next chapter will discuss these two concepts in more detail. They should not, however, be confused. Firms are *not* entrepreneurs, nor is the reverse the case. The modern received theory of the firm, however, virtually ignores this distinction. As a consequence it fails to take account of entrepreneurship and competition. It concentrates instead on equilibrium, a state where the entrepreneurial role is redundant, but which preserves a logical consistency, if not validity, in the received theory.

---

* The following paragraphs draw on I. Kirzener, 'Advertising', *The Freeman*, 1972.

REFERENCES

1 I. Kirzener, *Competition and Entrepreneurship*, University of Chicago Press 1974, pp. 6–7.
2 L. von Mises, *Human Action*, Regnery 1963, p. 254.
3 Mises, (1963), p.252.
4 Mises, (1963), pp. 246–50.
5 Mises, (1963), p.252.
6 J.A. Schumpeter, *Business Cycles*, Harrap 1939.
7 J.A. Schumpeter, *Capitalism, Socialism and Democracy*, Harrap 1948, p.88.
8 S.C. Littlechild, *Change Rules, O.K.?* University of Birmingham Press 1977, p.7.
9 G.L.S. Shackle, *Expectation, Enterprise and Profit*, George Allen and Unwin 1970, p. 106.
10 Kirzener, (1974), p.16.
11 Kirzener, (1974), p.48.
12 Robert Clower, private communication to Joan Robinson, cited in 'What are the questions?', *Journal of Economic Literature* 1977.
13 Kirzener, (1974), p. 144.
14 E.W. Clemens, 'Price discrimination and the multiple product firm,' *Review of Economic Studies* 1951.
15 D.L. Cocks, 'Product innovation and the dynamic elements of competition in the ethical pharmaceutical industry,' in R.B. Helms (ed.), *Drug Development and Marketing*, American Enterprise Institute 1975.
16 Kirzener (1974) , p.144.

. . . although economic activity encompasses both production (in the firm) and exchange (in the market), the concept of competition has been generally associated only with the latter.

Paul J. McNulty
Quarterly Journal of Economics, 1968.

7

Competition within the Firm

The terms 'entrepreneur' and 'firm' are sometimes wrongly regarded as synonymous. This is incorrect. The entrepreneur brings together resources into an entity known as the 'firm'. He then sells the output of these resources using the firm as his instrument of production. The firm comes into being at the instigation of the entrepreneur. In the course of time the original entrepreneur will go the way of all mortal flesh. The firm may die but need not. The firm can continue to survive earning a normal return and zero entrepreneurial profits. Alternatively, entrepreneurial elements within the firm may arise who either themselves earn rewards of a supra-normal level or who enable the firm (as represented by shareholders) to do so. The entrepreneur may own the firm or be employed by the firm, but the firm is not the entrepreneur.

(a) THE NATURE OF THE FIRM

It is easy to view the firm as a necessary accompaniment to large-scale production, specialisation and the division of labour. Surely production-line activity (for example) cannot be conducted by independent workers buying and selling from each other and renting floor space from a factory owner? Maurice Dobb argued that division of labour 'created the need for some integrating force without which differentiation would collapse into chaos'.[1]

Ronald Coase[2] argued that this was not so. There already is an 'integrating force' which avoids the postulated confusion. This force is the price system. With the price system, suppliers always have their customers' requirements in mind and rising or falling prices let them know what customers think of their product offerings. The relevant question is why on some occasions the integrating force is a firm, and on others it is a transaction carried out in the market?

Coase discounts the notion that it is the presence of uncertainty which is the reason for bringing firms into existence. All production is for speculative not certain demand. All production is entrepreneurial in nature. But the entrepreneurial role is not the same as the firm's role. Entrepreneurs can be, and are, hired in the market to undertake uncertainty. For example, speculators buy stock for unpredictable resale in the commodity futures market. Again the question is left unanswered: why in some cases does entrepreneurship coincide with a firm's activities, and in others is carried on at arm's length in the market place outside the firm?

Coase concluded that firms come into existence because the costs of using the price mechanism vary. Transactions are not homogeneous. When transaction costs rise too high, when the costs of negotiating and contracting become excessive, firms come into being. A firm then is merely that area of activity within which the economies of internal organisation exceed the economies of market relationships. To bring a firm into being, to assemble resources in anticipation of reduction in transactions costs is an entrepreneurial act. To maintain a firm in being need not be entrepreneurship.

The economies which can be obtained by replacing arms'

length relationships with firms are also limited. Many
arguments have been advanced since Austin Robinson
argued for the concept of the optimum sized firm.[3] Firms
are groups or teams of people (and other resources) and
groups must be coordinated. Coordination itself is not
costless and may be subject to diminishing returns.
Moreover, although firm or cooperative team production
may result in an output which exceeds the total output
which could be achieved by each team member if he
operated in isolation, and although this excess may be
greater than the costs of organising the firm or team,
there still remains the problem of monitoring.

Alchian and Demsetz[4] view the monitoring of effort
and the rewarding of productivity as the two major
problems in firm production. They argue that the interdependence of team production means that it is difficult
to ascertain what part of total output is attributable to any
one team member's efforts. Conversely, shirking may go
unobserved. In individual efforts the individual reaps all
the benefits of his efforts, and if he shirks he bears all the
costs of shirking. But in team work, the total costs of
shirking are not borne by the shirker, they are borne by
the full team. Everyone admits that he is better off if no
one shirks, but everyone also realises that if he alone shirks,
the cost to him will be small: he can get a 'free ride' on the
efforts of other team members.

More shirking will therefore occur in firms than in
individual market related transactions. Shirking is cheaper
in firms or teams and therefore each individual has a higher
incentive to substitute leisure for productive work. The
team members can get over the problem by hiring another
member to monitor the productive activity of the total
team. To be effective the monitor must have disciplinary
powers over shirkers which can be used without disbanding
the team. In short he must be able to fire a shirker. The
monitor watches and directs other team members by their
common consent. Any contract, express or implied, is
two-way. Whether the monitor initially hired the team or
the team initially hired him is irrelevant. Team members

enter into such contracts since they know a monitor is essential to maximise output. They want to maximise output since only in that way can they bargain for larger rewards when contracts come up for renegotiation.

Alchian and Demsetz then pose and attempt to answer the question: who monitors the monitor? How can team members ensure that he is diligent, that he does not shirk?

One way is to make him a residual claimant. All team members agree to work for a specific amount; any income remaining at the end of some arbitrary period is his. He is consequently motivated to make this residual as large as possible. The monitor can only have a residual claim if he has some form of property right. Alchian and Demsetz argue that the bundle of property rights listed in table 7.1 must be vested in the monitor.

Table 7.1 Property rights

(a)	To be a residual claimant
(b)	To observe input behaviour
(c)	To be the central party common to all contracts with inputs
(d)	To alter the membership of the team
(e)	To sell these rights

These rights represent the pattern of ownership of the traditional, entrepreneur-founded and controlled firm. Are they a valid description of the modern hierarchical corporation, where monitoring is carried on at a range of levels in the firm; where ownership is diffuse and divorced from control; and where the original founding entrepreneur has long since disappeared and identification of explicit entrepreneurial personnel in the firm is, at least to the outsider, apparently impossible? We will now try to answer these three questions in turn.*

(b) THE HIERARCHY AND THE EMPLOYMENT RELATION

Oliver Williamson[5] has presented the most widely developed

---

* For a full discussion of these issues see B. Chiplin and J. Coyne, *Can Workers Manage?* Institute of Economic Affairs 1977.

case for the emergence of complex hierarchical organisations. He emphasises that simple teams or organisations
where all workers are considered equal and where there is
no recognised authority have severe limitations.

Williamson's thesis commences by stressing the advantages of team activity over sequential spot contracting by
market exchange. Indivisible physical resources are used
for the maximum benefit of the group as a whole, and not
for the benefit of a monopolistic supplier renting out time
or space to individuals. Similarly, the learning-by-doing
informational advantages gained by team members on the
job accrue to the team as a whole. The costs of renegotiat-
ing with each worker (who is gaining ever more experience)
the terms under which he will supply his (ever changing
and ever scarcer) skills are eliminated or reduced. In brief,
transactions costs are reduced and all reap net benefits
individually as a consequence of team membership.

In addition, Williamson argues that simple, non-
hierarchical teams can offer a more certain income than
can individual effort coupled with insurance contracting
in the market. One reason for this assertion is that *ex ante*
recruitment to the team can limit membership to good
risks. That is, although selection errors will be made, a
policy of deliberately choosing or attempting to choose
productive, well-motivated co-workers will result in the
team being composed of members whose efficiency, on
average, is higher than that of all individuals in the market.
Insurance costs will consequently be lower in team effort
than in individual effort.

Finally, Williamson takes issue with Alchian and
Demsetz[4] that the benefits of team production as such,
namely the problem of non-separability of tasks, is why
groupings of workers emerge. Alchian and Demsetz use the
example of manhandling heavy loads into trucks which, to
be carried out efficiently, requires two men. Such examples
are alleged by Williamson to be rare or, if division of labour
by individual worker is not feasible, then division of labour
by small groupings certainly is. Take Smith's pin-making
example as an illustration. Each of the activities of wire

straightening, cutting, pointing, grinding and so on could be performed by an independent specialist or small group of specialists. Work could pass from process to process by purchase and sale. But buffer stocks would have to be held at each interval to facilitate coordination and so permit the drawing up of meaningful contracts to cover the exchanges made at each stage. Thus internal organisation comes about, Williamson argues, less because of the benefits of team production arising from non-separabilities as such (which is the Alchian and Demsetz view) but again (as with the Coase[2] approach) to minimise transactional costs (of haggling and of carrying relatively high inventories).

But why should peer group activity develop into hierarchical group activity? What are the specific costs which a non-hierarchical firm must meet, and what corresponding benefits accrue to a firm which removes its labour exchange activities from the extra-firm market to what Williamson calls the 'internal labour market'?

Williamson contends that non-hierarchical groups are limited by *'bounded rationality'*. In other words the human mind, even if it has an objectively rational goal, is unable to process all of the complex and voluminous information which is necessary in order to take the required decisions. The information can neither be adequately received, processed or transmitted. In the absence of hierarchy only two forms of communication are possible: the all-channel network or the wheel. Diagram 7.1 illustrates both forms of organisation.

The size of a non-hierarchical group of people is limited by the information-processing capacity of an all-channel

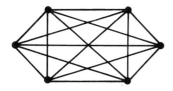

(a) All-channel network

(b) Wheel network

Diagram 7.1

network. The number of two-way flows in the all-channel case is given by the formula $n(n - 1)/2$, where n is the number of persons in the group (15 in the six-person case of diagram 7.1a). After a point the opportunity cost of wasted time by communicating everything to and from everyone for the purposes of reaching a collective decision becomes prohibitive. If scale economies of some type justify larger groupings of people then changes in organisational structure may be required.

Diseconomies of communication need not result in hierarchy, however. Communication economies can be still reaped, at least in smaller teams in peer group situations (as diagram 7.1b indicates). It is much simpler and cheaper for one person in a six-person case to take a decision and communicate it to the other five than for all six to reach a group decision. (In the wheel-network only $n - 1$, 5, communication flows are involved.) Provided only that there is no net reduction in the quality of decision reached, that everyone cooperates and that the group members take turns to act as the 'hub' of the wheel, then it is possible for a wheel network to persist without a hierarchy emerging.

A hierarchy will almost certainly emerge, however, because of 'bounded rationality *differentials*' between the members of the group. Williamson justifies this claim on the grounds that unless leadership of the group is undemanding, or each member is equally well qualified with respect to administration, then either group productivity or group democracy must be sacrificed.

Alchian and Demsetz argued that hierarchies would emerge because of the need to monitor the performance of the group and so minimise shirking. Williamson agrees with this and gives it as the second main reason for the limitations to peer group persistence. Malingerers, he argues, can be cajoled by their fellows to work harder; if that fails, rational appeals will be made; thirdly, the group will withdraw social benefits from the offender; and, finally, the group may resort to 'overt coercion and ostracism'. When these fail the free rider or shirker may be monitored and/or awarded discriminatory wages which is 'tantamount to introducing hierarchy'.

Once a hierarchy has emerged (*vis à vis* a non-hierarchical group) what benefits accrue? Williamson argues that the resulting structure, which in effect is what is commonly called the firm, is not rigidly authoritarian but is, in itself, an internal labour market, 'an employment relation', with distinct advantages over external labour markets.

Few internal labour markets would be rigidly authoritarian, however. Peer groupings do have the advantage of 'involvement'. Williamson argues that some individuals gain benefits from participation as such and that 'transparent inequality of rank (is) considered objectionable by some . . . (and) auditing and experience-rating may offend'. Thus the task of the leader of a hierarchy is '*to supply the requisite mixture of structures* . . . to allow individuals to match themselves to organisations in accordance with their involvement-productivity trade-offs'.

Not only do team members forfeit a degree of involvement when a hierarchy emerges; their property rights to specific tasks are also weakened once all tasks are placed, not only under common ownership, but under unilateral direction. (Income is more secure, as already pointed out, but the right to claim a *specific* job is less in a team situation than in an external labour market situation.) In order to understand the firm as an internal labour market (and so an entity which is not just a 'black box' but one to which economic or market analysis is applicable) it is necessary also to realise that, although property rights in specific tasks are relatively weak, '*job idiosyncrasy*' exists. Williamson argues that 'job idiosyncrasy' or non-homogeneity occurs because workers '*acquire*' during the course of their employment 'job-specific skills and related task-specific knowledge'.*

If property rights to jobs are weakened in a hierarchy

---

* This is comparable to the knowledge of the 'man-on-the-spot'. Compare Chapter 1, p.7.

then this mitigates against both the probability and possibility of market exchange in a firm. In turn, this may appear to preclude the use of economic analysis in the intra-firm situation. Conversely, workers progressively obtain more and more knowledge of the kind Hayek termed 'particular circumstances of time and place'. This results in asymmetry either in the information held by members of a firm and/or in the costs of acquiring that information. (Williamson defines this phenemenon as *'information impactedness'*.) But information impactedness is precisely the reason why normal market transactions occur. Entrepreneurs spot opportunities for mutually beneficial exchange between buyers and sellers, help initiate a suitable transaction and so move the market towards equilibrium.

In analogous manner, *within* the firm, the firm itself is moved towards its objective (or equilibrium) as members enter into mutually beneficial trades or contracts. Such exchanges occur, even in a hierarchical situation, because the parties to the exchange place different marginal valuations on the commodities (for simplicity, say labour and cash) they are trading. The differing marginal valuations arise due to information impactedness. The superior has unique information relating to the income the firm can obtain from a given set of productive inputs. The subordinate has unique know-how, arising from experience, relating to the task he will be called upon to perform. This makes it easier (i.e. cheaper) for him to perform that task at the margin and so makes it easier for him to compete against a willing but inexperienced subordinate (e.g. an outsider) who would have to incur training and learning costs.

Outsiders (outside the firm) can only achieve parity with insiders by first being taken on and then incurring these start-up costs. Incumbents are in possession of the valuable resource of on-the-job-experience and knowledge and can be expected only fully to reveal that know-how in exchange for something of value. Clearly, there is a danger that existing employees could enter into a series of bilateral monopoly deals with management, thus hurting the firm and employees elsewhere in the firm as well.

What kind of contractual relationship then is the most efficient? Williamson examines five. Only one is regarded as sufficiently flexible to permit adaptation to changing internal and external market circumstances. Only that one is also able to overcome the problems of opportunism (e.g. shirking), peer group organisation, and task idiosyncracy. That one is the internal labour market. We will initially survey the demerits of the other four.

First, a contract could be made now with a subordinate (or group of subordinates) to perform a specific task in the future. This, however, is impractical (i.e. too costly to implement) in complex and uncertain business environments and can be dismissed as of little practical interest. A second alternative is to draw the contract up in probabilistic or contingent terms to account for such uncertainties. An agreed wage would be paid now in return for future services which would depend on circumstances. Williamson argues that business life is too complex to write such employment contracts feasibly or cheaply *ex ante*. Bounded rationality would prohibit it. Even if it were feasible to write the contracts at reasonable expense, Williamson then argues that there would be problems of comprehensibility which would impede agreement. At least one party to the contract (probably the worker) would not fully understand the ramifications of the complex agreement to which he is being asked to accede. Information impactedness would be an obstacle. *Ex post*, the contract would face enormous enforcement problems. Opportunism could result in shirking. Information impactedness could result in disputes over which contingent state of the world had, in fact, come to pass. And resort to arbitration would not, by definition, reduce the information impactedness problem. The arbitrator himself would face the problem as to how much of the apparent or claimed knowledge asymmetry regarding the state of the world was real and how much was due to opportunism (lack of candour or honesty in drawing up or executing the transaction).

The third alternative is sequential contracting. Alchian and Demsetz[4] view the firm and the apparent long-term association between employer and employee *not* as a continuing authoritative relationship but as a series of short-term contracts in the spot market. This concept permits continuous adaptation of the contract to changing circumstances and so overcomes the problems of uncertainty. Bounded rationality and information impactedness pose much less severe problems since no attempt is made to detail all contingencies in advance and so, *ex post*, there need be no dispute over which state of the world had come to pass. Williamson, however, denies that sequential spot contracting can be applied to the situation of the firm because of unacceptably high transaction costs. It is an inefficient contractual mode. Its inefficiency lies in the scope for opportunistic behaviour due to task idiosyncracy. This 'effectively destroys parity (with outsiders) at the contract renewal interval. Incumbents who enjoy non-trivial advantages over similarly qualified but inexperienced bidders are well-situated to demand some fraction of the cost savings which their idiosyncratic experience has generated'. This problem is attenuated only in these industries where high labour turnover does not impose high costs — Williamson cites migratory farm workers as an example — but such examples are rare. Unless this condition is achieved then problems of opportunism can only be overcome if workers are either asked to bid for employment contracts by offering lump sums to employers reflecting the present value of the monopoly gains which will accrue to them due to their idiosyncratic experience (but this reintroduces issues of bounded rationality and information impactedness); or if workers promise not to behave opportunistically when contracts come up for renegotiation, which assumes they will behave irrationally; or if workers submit to some form of monitoring, which Alchian and Demsetz view as comparable with sequential spot contracting as they interpret it, but which Williamson would argue is close to the authority relation.

The fourth contractual relationship is that of authority. Williamson paraphrased Simon's[7] definition of the employment contract. Such an agreement exists if a worker is willing to accept a boss's authority in exchange for a stated wage. This type of agreement will be preferred to an extra-firm 'sales contract' provided that a deterministic (wholly certain) sales contract cannot be drawn up and that the area of uncertainty which does remain (what the worker will, in fact, be asked to do) will not prove unattractive to the worker. It will be advantageous to the boss to draw up such a contract if he wishes to postpone the precise selection of the worker's task until some time after the contract is made. Simon's authority contract is simply one in which the parties 'agree to tell and be told'. But, Williamson argues, 'the terms are rigged from the outset'. The 'sales contract' with which Simon compares his authority relation is merely our first contractual (and flexible) alternative. Our second and third possibilities (a contingent sales contract and a series of sequential spot contracts) both offered the advantages of flexibility in response to changing circumstances. Does the authority relation, then, offer anything in terms of efficiency? It is less costly than the contingent sales contract in that it does not impose the bounded rationality problem and so high transaction costs of generating knowledge of all alternatives outcomes in advance. It is superior to the spot contracting mode in that transaction costs are lowered due to the decrease in frequency with which contracts are negotiated. Nevertheless, all of the problems of task idiosyncracy which were present in spot contracting remain to be faced. For example, how are terms of employment to be adjusted over time as circumstances change? How are the problems of disputes due to either opportunism or information impactedness to be resolved? With job idiosyncracy firms will either have to bear the high costs of continuous labour turnover or the high costs of meeting the demands of idiosyncratic workers with monopoly bargaining power.

The fifth possibility, the internal labour market is, if not optimal in terms of minimising transactions costs between firms and employees, possibly the closest approach to optimality yet suggested. In particular, it overcomes the problems posed by task idiosyncracies. The essence of the employment relation or the internal labour market is that the individual contract is replaced by the collective bargain. This results, to cite Williamson, in a 'fundamental transformation ... where wage rates are attached mainly to jobs rather than to workers'. The incentive to behave opportunistically which individual workers would have in individual contracting (due to their peculiar experience) is thus greatly reduced. The collective agreement also overcomes problems of uncertainty by being written in general terms which makes it 'an instrument of government as well as exchange'.

All individuals who collectively accede to the contract presumably do so because they feel it is to their individual net advantages. Each has an area within which he is indifferent as to what instruction he may receive from those to whom he has granted authority or powers of government. But any one individual whose area of indifference is opportunistically distinct from those of the rest of the group will not, provided the distinction is small, reject authority. Should he do so he would pose a threat to the benefits of all the other individuals who gain from the agreement. Thus group pressures would be exerted against such opportunistic behaviour and the authority relationship embodied in the contract be reinforced from below.

Bounded rationality is attenuated by writing the contract in non-precise terms. Information impactedness, *ex post*, or disagreements in contractual interpretation resulting in disputes, are provided for by writing into the contract, *ex ante*, details of dispute-settling mechanisms. This allows the day-to-day running of the firm to be pursued while the grievance is tackled by the arbitration apparatus devised by the parties to the contract. Since this apparatus may be composed of some sort of elected group (such as a union committee) representing the workers as a whole, it will be more concerned with the interests of the total labour force. Thus, again, opportunistic behaviour due to task idiosyncracy is curbed.

But the acceptance of the employment relation does not ensure that the firm receives 'consummate' as opposed to 'perfunctory' cooperation from its labour force. The former is described by Williamson as an 'affirmative job attitude' including the 'use of judgement, filling gaps, and taking initiative in an instrumental way'. The latter, by contrast 'involves job performance of a minimally acceptable sort — where minimally acceptable means that incumbents who have idiosyncratic advantages, 'need merely to maintain a slight margin over the best available inexperienced candidate'.

Consummate cooperation could be obtained by awarding individual incentive payments of a sequential spot contract kind but this is precluded in the collective bargains of internal labour markets. Williamson argues instead that the advantages of internal labour markets can be maintained, but consummate cooperation also obtained, if, as part of the internal incentive system, higher level positions are generally filled by internal promotions. If such practices are followed by most firms the internal labour market is strengthened.

Other implications follow. The firm can risk avert by only employing newcomers at low levels in the hierarchy. This protects the firm against opportunistic job applicants who might represent themselves as more productive than they otherwise are. Promotion will only follow as experience warrants it. Restricting 'ports of entry' to low level jobs reflects the advantages of the internal market over the external labour market in other ways as well. Any lateral transfer which could occur between firms at higher levels because an employee is motivated to move due to a (correct) denial of promotion in his original firm is less likely. Interim information impactedness might otherwise have resulted in such a transfer taking place. The new employer would not have had the advantage of the old employer's hierarchy to provide him with information relating to the defects of the new entrant. Moreover, opportunism by the old employer could have resulted in problems of veracity regarding the quality of the new entrant. The old employer might have been only too happy to be rid of the employee (who might have reached his existing level in the old firm as a consequence of a rating error in the first place).

In short, intra-firm labour markets, hierarchies, have informational advantages over extra-firm labour markets. They are less subject to bounded rationality, information impactedness, and to opportunistic behaviour. They are better than perfunctory cooperation as a consequence of their hierarchical structure. And a monitor, indeed a hierarchy of monitors, in the Alchian and Demsetz sense, is still required.

But whereas the latter resign themselves to team production, and the consequent inseparability of production functions, the former do not. Alchian and Demsetz[4] argue that 'measuring *marginal* productivity and making payment in accord therewith' is too expensive and so the monitor allocates rewards on the basis of observed *input* behaviour thus minimising shirking. Williamson,[5] however, while admitting that 'although the attachment of wages to jobs rather than individuals may result in an imperfect correspondence between wages and marginal productivity at ports of entry, productivity differentials will be recognised ... and a more perfect correspondence can be expected for higher-level assignments in the internal labour market job hierarchy'.

(c) THE OBJECTIVES OF THE FIRM AND THE MARKET FOR CORPORATE CONTROL

While it could be argued that the modern hierarchical corporation has vested in it some of the property rights listed in table 7.1, there are others in that list for which such a claim can less easily be made. In the preceding pages we have seen how the monitor at various levels of the firm can exercise the rights of observation, centrality in contracting, and the ability to alter team membership (points (ii), (iii) and (iv) in table 7.1) by virtue of the employment relation, promotion, and in the ultimate, the ability to fire an unsatisfactory team member. We have also seen that the internal labour market, the firm, can be more efficient, on occasion, than external contracting; a view perfectly in accord with Coase's arguments based on transactions costs.[1]

But how can we claim that in modern large-scale enterprises, where ownership is divorced from control, that points (i) and (v) are fulfilled? It is the shareholder who is the legal residual claimant and who has the legal right to sell his ownership title, yet control is vested in the managerial hierarchy. Diffused ownership, the minimal impact of one shareholder, and the implied rise in policing costs reduce the element of control.

Nevertheless, to restore shareholder control — or alternatively to illustrate that divorce from ownership is more apparent than real — it is merely necessary to illustrate that directors and managers can be and are subject to outside discipline. Domestic competition — provided it is not mitigated by government subsidy — is one such disciplinary device. Foreign competition — provided it is not eroded by tariff or other protection — is another. Finally, the market for corporate control (the take-over mechanism) provides potentially one of the most substantial disciplines on managerial discretion. (Although again a *caveat* must be entered given that the liquidation of large enterprises is a rarity whose exceptional nature is enhanced by government 'lame-duck' policies; a phenomenon particularly prevalent in Britain.)

Robin Marris's[8] work is seminal in the literature on the take-over mechanism, and has been subject to diagrammatic exposition by Radice.[9] We will draw on these two authors to illustrate our discussion.

Shareholders are assumed to have as their objective wealth maximisation. This is defined as the present value of the stream of future dividends they will receive plus the present value of their shares on date of ultimate realisation. In equation form this can be expressed as:

$$V_0 = \sum_{t=1}^{n} \frac{D_t}{(1+r)^t} + \frac{V_n}{(1+r)^n} \qquad (1)$$

where V_0 is today's share price, D_t is the dividend per share received in year t and V_n is the share price in year n. But since V_n can be rewritten as:

$$V_n = \sum_{t = n+1}^{\infty} \frac{D_t}{(1 + r)^t}$$

then equation (1) simplifies to:

$$V_0 = \sum_{t = 1}^{\infty} \frac{D_t}{(1 + r)^t}$$

Managers, on the other hand, are assumed to have the objective of maximising the rate of growth of the firm subject only to a security constraint. How are the two objectives, corporate growth and corporate stock market value, related? Marris argues that there is a two-way relationship between corporate growth and profitability. In equation form:

$$g = f (\pi) \tag{2}$$

and $\pi = \phi (g)$ \hfill (3)

where g is rate of growth and π is profitability. Equation (2) in its specified version would indicate that growth varies directly with profitability. In essence, profits are the source of growth. It represents the supply of capital constraint on growth. Without profits internal financing of growth is not possible, and without the prospect of profits external financing either by borrowing or the issue of new equity is also impossible. The higher are profits, conversely, the higher is the rate of growth which can be pursued.

Equation (3), if specified, would indicate that profitability first rises with corporate growth then falls. One dynamic model of the firm, first described by Baumol, highlights this point. Consider diagram 7.2.

The TC function is composed of two types of cost: output costs and expansion costs. Output costs are the

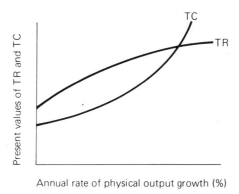

Annual rate of physical output growth (%)

Diagram 7.2

ordinary, day-to-day operating and production costs. They
are composed of fixed and variable costs; and if we assume
constant returns to scale they will rise in a linear fashion as
the firm's annual rate of growth rises. (If the firm has
identified the optimum scale of plant, it can replicate that
plant as often as required to meet any output growth
needs.) On the other hand, expansion costs can be expected
to rise more than proportionately as the rate of growth
increases. It is for this reason that the TC function is displaying non-linear properties. One major reason for the
disproportionate rise in expansion costs is the limited
ability of management to administer efficiently a growing
entity. Growth entails recruitment of new personnel at all
levels of the firm. These must be trained and assimilated
into the organisation. While new staff are being trained and
gaining experience inefficiencies arise. The greater the
training task and the more employees there are then,
given the fixed size of the original management team, the
higher these inefficiencies become, and the firm's expansion
costs rise accordingly. This is exactly what would be
expected from the earlier discussion on the relative efficiency of internal versus external labour markets. If
expansion implies that the firm must open ports of entry
both more widely and at hierarchical levels other than the
lowest, then costs of bounded rationality, information
impactedness and opportunism would be incurred at

relatively high levels. Expansion costs also rise disproportionately if the firm tries to shorten the time required to
construct new fixed-plant capacity. 'Crash programmes'
invariably raise unit costs. Also, ever more rapid growth
requires ever more capital to finance the expansion. Beyond
some level, the cost of capital will rise. For example,
frequent issues of shares to raise funds will force the price
of equity down and so its cost of servicing up.

The TR function will most probably rise, at least at
first, as the rate of growth of output rises above zero.
However, although output can be raised by any or all of
price reductions, advertising, and diversification, it is very
probable that after some point each of these tactics will
encounter diminishing returns. Thus the TR curve will,
after that point, increase at a decreasing rate.

As a consequence of this reasoning, equation (3) if
graphed would be shaped like an inverted U, and equation
(2) would rise, as a straight line passing through the origin.
This is illustrated in diagram 7.3. The firm can then locate
anywhere within the shaded area.

The precise positioning of the supply of capital line
merits further explanation. Its location is dependent on
the subjective preferences of the management for security
of tenure. If they are risk-averse the line will be pivoted
further to the left; if they are risk-preferring it will be
pivoted further to the right. The rationale for this statement is that given any level of profitability, then the rate
at which growth can proceed is dependent on dividend

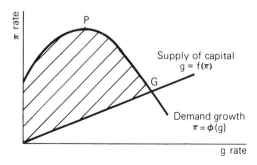

Diagram 7.3

distribution levels, new borrowing requirements or new issues of equity. Each of these sources of finance is finite. If retention levels rise above a certain level either shareholders' time preference patterns will result in them preferring dividends today rather than increased dividends and capital gains tomorrow, or managers will engage in extramarginal projects, thus reducing the future earnings yield.

If this process is carried too far shareholders will sell their shares and share prices will fall. Similarly, if the company borrows heavily it may become too highly geared for existing shareholders' preferences. They will sell shares and again the market value of the firm will fall. A similar result occurs if firms issue new equity in order to engage in extra-marginal ventures. 'Dilution' of existing shareholders' earnings occurs and the market price of their shares will fall.

Any or all of these consequences of growth leading to a lower share price could, according to Marris, encourage a 'take-over raid' which, if successful, would jeopardise the jobs of the managers who opted for a policy of growth in the first instance. In consequence, the security preferences of the management determine the slope of the supply of capital line.

A low share price will attract a take-over raider. But a firm's share price or market value (where market value is share price times the number of issued shares) is an absolute measure and depends on the size of the firm (and the number of shares issued). Marris uses a relative measure, the 'valuation ratio', to ascertain whether or not a firm's share price is high or low in terms of attractiveness to a take-over raider. The valuation ratio is defined as the ratio of total market value of all the firm's shares to the book value of the firm's assets measured at replacement cost.

After a point, Marris argues, if a company pursues growth, profitability falls, market value falls and so the valuation ratio declines. If the valuation ratio declines far enough a raid will occur. This point is reached when the actual valuation ratio falls below the subjective valuation ratio put on the firm by a potential bidder. In short, a firm will be taken over if a buyer believes he can make more productive use of the existing assets than can the existing management team.

This argument is illustrated in diagram 7.3. Point P is the optimum operating point if shareholders are interested only in current dividends. Somewhere to the right of P is optimal if shareholders wish to maximise wealth. Point G is optimal for growth orientated managers; it maximises the firm's growth rate at a level consistent with the minimum valuation ratio embodied in the position of the supply of capital line.

Diagram 7.4 presents the same arguments in a more explicit form. Point X indicates the point of maximum shareholder satisfaction given that they wish to maximise their wealth and so make some trade-off between current dividends and capital gains. At point X equation (1) is maximised, share price is at its highest possible level and thus by definition so also is the firm's valuation ratio (as

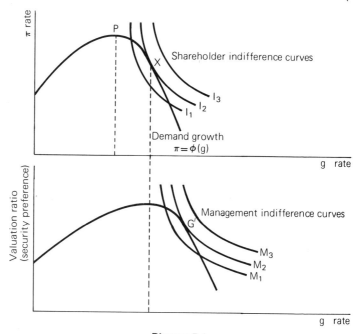

Diagram 7.4

indicated by the lower half of diagram 7.4). Managers too, however, are in a trade-off situation. They are not, like shareholders, comparing current dividends with future dividends, but rather job security against corporate growth. Their indifference curves are indicated by the lines labelled M_1, M_2 and M_3. Given the indifference curves of the diagram, the managers of the firm will choose point G' and the appropriate growth-rate/valuation-ratio combination. (G' in diagram 7.4 implies the same growth rate as G in diagram 7.3.)

However, managerial utility (M) is a function of security (the valuation ratio), and if the threat of take-over is high enough, the indifference curves labelled M will be close to horizontal and G' and X will coincide vertically (in diagram 7.4) (and in diagram 7.3) and the supply-of-capital line will pivot to the left maintaining the implication that G and G' still result in equal growth rates.

To summarise, provided what Manne[11] termed the market in 'corporate control' is working effectively, then it can be presumed that managers are disciplined to act in shareholders interests. If this is so then all five of the property rights listed in table 7.1 are vested in the shareholder as monitor. Some of the activities implied by these rights are delegated to directors, managers and executives through the various levels of the hierarchy. This implies, however, less a divorce of ownership from control and more a marriage of convenience between internal labour markets and entrepreneurship.

(d) ENTREPRENEURSHIP

Marriage partners, however, as the Bible tells us 'are no more twain, but are one flesh'. In analytic or legalistic terms it may in many situations be impossible to distinguish husband from wife. So, analogously, in the marriage of convenience which is the modern corporation it may be impossible to ascertain who the entrepreneur is.

Von Mises[12] argues that the entrepreneurial function

can exist at all levels in the hierarchical firm, but warns that it is a serious error to confuse the entrepreneur with any particular category in the hierarchy. 'The manager is a junior partner of the entrepreneur . . . (whose) own financial interests force him to attend to the best of his abilities to the entrepreneurial functions which are assigned to him within a limited and precisely determined sphere of action.' In a firm which is subject to what Mises terms 'profit management', entrepreneurship can be delegated. Profit centres can be set up within a business and the entrepreneur can allocate tasks to each and appraise each centre according to the profits it contributes to the total business. Each division can be regarded as an autonomous business buying and selling to other divisions and to the outside market. Thus the entrepreneur can assign to each section's management a great deal of independence. Within circumscribed limits divisional managers need merely to be told to make as much profit as possible. 'Every manager and sub-manager is responsible for the working of his section or sub-section . . . If he incurs losses, he will be replaced . . . If he succeeds in making profits his income will be increased, or at least he will not be in danger of losing it . . . His task is not like that of the technician, to perform a definite piece of work according to a definite precept. It is to adjust — within the limited scope left to his discretion — the operation of his section to the state of the market'.

Thus employees in a firm at any level in the hierarchy can exercise an entrepreneurial role. The area within which that role can be carried out increases the more authority the employee has. But the manager, no matter how high, can never be the entrepreneur since he 'cannot be made answerable for the losses incurred'. In the final analysis, Mises argues, the entrepreneur is the owner. He alone determines the grand strategy of the business. He may call on managerial advice but the decisions are his. Decisions as to 'what lines of business to employ capital (in) and how much capital to employ . . . (decisions as to) expansion and contraction of the size of the total business, and its main sections . . . (decisions as to its) financial structure' fall upon the entrepreneur alone.

The mechanism used to ensure this is the market for corporate control, the stock market. The prices of stocks and shares 'are the means applied by the capitalists for the supreme control of the flow of capital . . . (this) decides how much capital is available for the conduct of each corporation's business; it creates a state of affairs to which the managers must adjust their operations in detail'.*

Not only is this a positivist description of the industrial firm it is also, Mises argues, normatively desirable. 'Society can freely leave the care for the best possible employment of capital goods to their owners. In embarking upon definite projects these owners expose their own property, wealth and social position. They are even more interested in . . . success . . . than is society as a whole. For society as a whole the squandering of capital invested in a definite project means only the loss of a small part of its total funds; for the owner it means much more . . . But if a manager is given a completely free hand, things are different. He speculates in risking other people's money. He sees the prospects of an uncertain enterprise from another angle than that of the man who is answerable for the losses . . . he becomes foolhardy because he does not share in the losses too.'

Thus, the entrepreneurial function can be partially delegated. In the ultimate, however, the entrepreneur himself remains the owner of the property rights detailed in table 7.1. To ensure that he retains these property rights the market in corporate control must be subject to effective

---

* What if, as a matter of empirical fact, shareholders lack the power to fire management? What if, as a consequence, managers pursue their own objectives (and presumably do so as entrepreneurs in their own right but use their alertness to spot opportunities which will benefit themselves and the firm) and are persistently able to do so? This is a cost to shareholders. 'If in the light of this known cost . . . (the shareholder persists in doing business with the manager) . . . we must conclude that in his *entrepreneurial* judgement the cost is worthwhile.' (Kirzener, op.cit. p. 65)

competition. The divorce of ownership from control must, if society is to be optimally served by the entrepreneurial function, be a fiction. The reality should be a marriage of convenience between the internal labour market and the entrepreneur.

(e) ENTREPRENEURSHIP, MANAGEMENT AND BUREAUCRACY

The notion that the entrepreneurial function can exist at any level in the hierarchical firm is emphasised by Mises when he contrasts 'profit management' with 'bureaucratic management'. The latter 'is the method applied in the conduct of administrative affairs, the result of which has no cash value in the market'. Under profit management considerable authority is delegated and so flexibility permitted. The lower levels are expected to know the condition of supply and demand, the particular markets, far better than managers at the top level can possibly know them. Thus there is an integration of knowledge. The top level assigns the general goals while the lower levels attempt to fulfil these goals as profitably as possible. If they succeed they are left alone or rewarded; if they fail they can inform the upper levels of any corrections needed in overall goals, or else they can be replaced. Their income is therefore dependent on success or failure in the market.

Bureaucratic management operates under a totally different method of financing. Expenses are met by the state; thus the responsibility of managers is to see to it that all income received is spent only on those items budgeted for in advance and approved by the sponsor. The discretion of the managers at the various hierarchical levels is not restricted by considerations of profit or loss. They cannot be given the self-understood instruction which need not even be articulated: make profits. If bureaucratic managers were to be given total freedom of action they would do what they wanted, not what their bosses or the people wanted. Mises argues that to 'prevent this outcome...

it is necessary to give them detailed instructions regulating their conduct of affairs in every respect'. The task of the upper level is supervisory, not in the sense of evaluating profit and loss but in the sense of control. Accurate reporting of control data is at a premium: the goal is total *predictability*.

Predictability as a goal, and the bureaucratic management which aims for it and of itself necessitates it, is neither desirable nor undesirable *per se*. Mises argued that bureaucratic management is indispensable to the conduct of affairs which have no cash value on the market. There, profit management is impossible. Entrepreneurship, decision-taking activity to profitably meet the anticipated, but *uncertain,* future demands of consumers, can have no place in an organisation with no cash nexus and a control system which rests on *predictability and certainty*.

Human beings, however, are motivated by self interest. In a profit-management organisation subject to the takeover threat, this will display itself in entrepreneurial action. As Mises argued, no 'business, whatever its size or specific task, can ever become bureaucratic so long as it is entirely and solely operated on a profit basis'. Should a firm abandon profit-seeking due to an imperfect market in corporate control, however, then bureaucratic management methods will be substituted.

Later writers have developed the analysis still further. For example Niskanen[13] agrees that there is an important difference between the exchange relation of a public service agency or bureau and that of a market-orientated firm. The bureau offers an all-or-nothing package instead of separate units of services at a price. But Niskanen goes beyond Mises and argues that not only does this preclude entrepreneurial adjustment to the needs of the market, but it also gives it a bargaining power akin to that of a monopoly — profit maximising by discriminating between customers. This results in the bureau producing an output of services larger than a private monopolist would supply. The latter maximises profit, the former maximises total revenue subject to its budget. Diagram 7.5 illustrates this

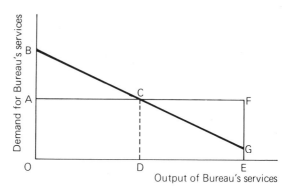

Diagram 7.5

argument and shows how the bureau is able to expand output well beyond the competitive ($P = MC$) level.

A competitive industry would produce OD, yielding net consumer benefits of ABC. A bureau, however, because of its all-or-nothing terms of supply and so monopoly bargaining power with politicians (the consumers' elected representatives), can obtain for itself this consumers' surplus. The surplus represents the difference between what consumers (i.e. taxpayers) would be prepared to pay for the good rather than go without the amount bought at the market price. The bureau will, therefore, be able to expand its budget until its output equals OE, twice the optimum, where CFG = ABC. This is the 'budget-constrained' case where total revenue or budget (OBGE) just covers total costs (OAFE). In the 'demand-constrained' case (diagram 7.6) bureaux promote their services, shift demand to the right and reduce its elasticity. The bureau will eventually reach a point where the marginal evaluation of its services is zero. In this case the budget (OBE) will equal costs (OAFE) at output level E. Neither situation is optimal, and of the two the less preferred is the demand constrained case. (In diagram 7.6 the ratio of total benefits to total costs for producing the excess output DE is CDE : CDEF. This is less than the corresponding ratio CDEG : CDEF in diagram 7.5.)

Profit managed firms consequently foster entrepreneurship at all levels. The servicing of consumer needs, actual and potential, is a priority and meeting that objective results in entrepreneurial reward. Given the uncertainty involved in the estimation of current and future demand, flexibility is a *sine qua non* at all levels in profit managed organisations. In bureaucratic organisations rigidity of management style is necessary to ensure that consumers do not suffer from opportunism on the part of management below the topmost level. Rigidity of control, however, may not be sufficient to ensure that the incentive for personal gain, which is present in all human beings, does not result in bureaucratic output being expanded beyond the level which the public or consumer would wish. The self-interest which in one case can result in opportunities for creative, consumer-serving, entrepreneurial activity at all levels in a firm can, in the other, result in unwanted levels of 'service' or red tape. In the former, self-interest is channelled into entrepreneurial activity by the casting of a myriad of daily votes by consumers through market transactions. In the latter, self-interest is (rightly) curbed on a daily basis by rigid control; but is only curbed (and that inadequately) on an overall scale by infrequent and probably indecisive polling of the electorate.

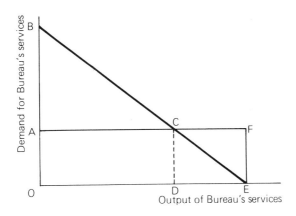

Diagram 7.6

REFERENCES

1 Cited in R.H. Coase, 'The nature of the firm', *Economica* 1937.
2 R.H. Coase (1937).
3 E.A.G. Robinson, *The Structure of Competitive Industry*, Cambridge 1931.
4 A. Alchian and A. Demsetz, 'Production, information costs, and economic organisation', *American Economic Review* 1972.
5 O.E. Williamson, *Markets and Hierarchies, Analysis and Antitrust Implications*, The Free Press 1975, Chapters 3 and 4.
6 F.A. Hayek, 'The use of knowledge in society', *American Economic Review* 1945.
7 H.A. Simon, *Models of Man*, Wiley 1957.
8 R. Marris, *The Economics of Managerial Capitalism*, Macmillan 1964.
9 H. Radice, 'Control type, profitability and growth in large firms: an empirical study', *Economic Journal* 1971.
10 W.J. Baumol, 'On the theory of expansion of the firm', *American Economic Review* 1962.
11 H.G. Manne, 'Mergers and the market for corporate control', *Journal of Political Economy* 1965.
12 L. von Mises, *Human Action* (3rd edition), Regnery 1966, pp. 303–311.
13 W.A. Niskanen, *Bureaucracy and Representative Government*, Aldine-Atherton 1971.

*. . . competition is a process of discovering new and better
ways of doing things, spurred on by the lure of profit.*

S.C. Littlechild, *Inaugural Lecture, Birmingham
University*, 1977

*Monopoly . . . means . . . the position of a producer whose
exclusive control over necessary inputs blocks competitive
entry . . . (it) does not refer to the . . . only producer of a
particular product . . . since other entrepreneurs are entirely free to compete with him.*

Israel Kirzener, *Competition and Entrepreneurship*, 1973

8

Concluding Thoughts

This is not the kind of text which readily lends itself to a
conventional neat summary of conclusions in the final
chapter. No such collection of pronouncements can be
justified from a superficial investigation into a long neglected but recently resurgent theory, where historic data
have supported more universally acceptable paradigms and
only lately have those data been seriously challenged.
Moreover the whole topic of industrial organization is
encyclopaedic in nature.

The subject could have been approached wholly empirically using cross-sectional or time series analyses of data on
prices, profits and other economic variables. Alternatively
case-by-case industry studies could have been carried out
and the behaviour of industries and firms analysed in depth.
This text could also have been written as a conventional
'theory of the firm' or 'price theory' volume. Equally
legitimately, the public policies of government towards
business in either or both of the USA and the UK could

have been studied. Whole libraries exist on anti-trust laws and cases, on government price controls and on other forms of official intervention in industrial activity.

Alternatively, a normative approach could have been adopted as in my *Managerial Economics* laying down rules showing firms how to maximise profits. Conversely, the concept of the 'social audit' could have been used and the behaviour of industries and firms could have been judged by their ability to meet some predetermined 'social' objective other than profit.

Instead the above pages have summarised some of the challenges to determinism,* whether that determinism was of neoclassical or of Marxian orthodoxy. They have explicitly rejected neoclassical equilibrium theory and implicitly denied dialectical materialism.†

Given all of this, it is not surprising that this book poses many more questions than it answers, and is generally concerned more with breaking down myths than with the construction or elaboration of the Austrian theory. It has looked at standard price theory and found it wanting both on a factual basis and, often, even in logic. To this extent it is a negative book, but one perhaps on which to build. A number of issues have been raised.

(a) THE OPTIMAL FIRM AND THE KALEIDIC SOCIETY?

In rigid neoclassical orthodoxy equilibrium already prevails in conditions of perfect competition. In Austrian eco-

---

* Determinism is the doctrine that man is not a free agent but that his actions are determined by conditions independent of his will.

† The Marxian concept that the inherent logic of 'material productive forces' propels society via the class struggle towards socialism 'with the inexorability of a law of nature'. Conditions of production — 'material productive forces' — were facts to Marx, independent of but determining human thought and action. 'The handmill gives you society with a feudal lord; the steam mill, society with the industrial capitalist.' (From *The Poverty of Philosophy*, p. 105. This was the nearest Marx got to defining a 'material productive force'.)

nomics the market process *potentially* terminates in a state
of long-run general equilibrium. But in what Shackle[1] called
a 'Kaleidic Society' there are always sooner or later unexpected changes which upset existing patterns, 'interspersing
its moments or intervals of order, assurance and beauty with
sudden disintegration and a cascade into a new pattern'.
Hence in real-life industry, where changes in technologies
and consumer tastes occur, but where much capital equipment is durable and specific, the equilibrating force of the
entrepreneur is always overtaken before it has done its
work. Individual markets for individual goods may, for a
time, find their respective equilibria, but the economic
system never does. The prospect of an optimum firm
monopolising an entire industry may always appear to be
present; on occasion it may actually exist. In reality it
cannot be a pervasive phenomenon, nor can it be a persistent
one.

(b) SUBJECTIVISM AND EQUILIBRIUM?

To the extent that the theory of perfectly competitive
equilibrium is based on a subjective demand curve it rests
on an illogicality. The subjective theory of value holds that
the value of economic goods is in the minds of individual
men and therefore is neither constant nor inherent in the
goods themselves; values of the same goods vary, as the
judgements of the individuals making the valuations vary,
from person to person and from time to time for the same
person. Individual valuations vary as underlying tastes
change. Subjective valuations vary even if tastes do not
change. The price on the vertical axis of the demand curves
is *relative* price not absolute cash price (that is, it represents
in money terms what must be given up, on average, of other
goods to obtain varying amounts of the commodity in
question per unit of time). If this is so and if the stock of
commodities which an individual has is continuously
changing (since consumption and replenishment via production are unlikely to exactly match in a monetary

economy where individuals work for cash and do not barter) then the valuation placed by individuals on any particular class of items in their total stock of commodities will vary over time according to the principle of diminishing marginal utility. This in turn will affect the relative price of any commodity whether or not the individual's stock of *that* commodity has changed, and whether or not the individual's underlying preferences for *that* commodity remain the same. It is this 'subjective use-value' and 'the preference given to *a* over *b*' which determines 'the formation of prices'.[2] As tastes change, as stocks change, as 'the preference given to *a* over *b*' changes, consumer demands change and deriving an equilibrium theory from a continuously fluid demand function is a straight *non sequitur*.

(c) WORKABLE COMPETITION AND THE S/C/P PARADIGM AGAIN

In recent years other critics of the structure/conduct/performance (S/C/P) paradigm have appeared. One of the earliest and most thoughtful of these was J.M. Clark who adopted the phrase 'workable competition'.[3] He argues that competition is essentially dynamic and that because of this 'the imperfectly competitive mixed economy we have is better than the impossible abstraction of' perfectly competitive equilibrium.[4]

Some 20 years after Clark's first paper, S.M. Sosnick summarised the progress of 'workable' or 'effective' competition in the light of later writings and against the background of the S/C/P framework. Sosnick's schema is summarised in table 8.1. The table, however, while encapsulating the views of those such as Clark who are dissatisfied with the standard writings on industrial organisation, is little more than a string of non-operational platitudes. Most of the criteria are too indefinite and are open to widely varying subjective interpretations. Moreover, the first two structural norms closely approach the requirements of perfect competition. To the extent that they do then the remainder of the table is redundant.*

Clark perceived this in his last book. Not only must an analysis of static equilibrium rightly be seen as simply a means to the end of a study of dynamic competition but 'something more' is required.[5] This 'something more' requires a 'fresh equipment of dynamic tools . . . which will introduce into such basic concepts as demand . . . and cost . . . the element of time, change over time and especially the processes involved in the initiation of changes and adjustment to them, including anticipations and uncertainties.' Clark was making an unconscious plea for a study of a catallaxy. Unfortunately he advanced little further than an expansion (albeit masterly) of table 8.1.

More recently Sir John Hicks[6] has made a similar implied plea for an investigation of catallactics rather than equilibrium. He observed that the very concept of equilibrium arose from a misleading analogy with movements in space, which cannot be applied to movements in time. In space one can go back and forth. In time there is only one way to go. Mistakes cannot be corrected nor an equilibrium reached by trial and error. Since the sum of all individual choices is based upon more or less independent and inaccurate judgements about what the outcome will be, it is impossible that they should be mutually consistent.

If they were then prices would equal marginal costs and monopoly profits would be zero. This is the situation traditional neo-classical theory described as 'optimal'. From this theory has sprung the market concentration doctrine which has been shown above to have either weak empirical underpinnings or, and more probably, to be empirically invalid.

The essential difference between the S/C/P paradigm and catallactics from a welfare viewpoint is that the S/C/P model has a social welfare objective predefined ($P=MC$) while a catallactic approach does not and cannot. The S/C/P model and the market concentration doctrine have proved

---

* See also the discussion of Sosnick in Scherer (1970).

Table 8.1 Workable competition and the structure/
conduct/performance paradigm

Structural Norms

   (i)   Number of traders to be as large as scale economies permit.
  (ii)   No artificial inhibitions to mobility or entry.
 (iii)   Moderate and price sensitive quality differentials in the products offered.

Conduct Criteria

   (i)   Some uncertainty should exist in the minds of rivals as to whether price
       initiatives will be followed.
  (ii)   Goals to be striven for independently, i.e. no collusion.
 (iii)   No unfair, exclusionary, predatory or coercive tactics.
 (iv)   Inefficient suppliers and customers should not be permanently shielded.
  (v)   Promotion should not mislead.
 (vi)   Persistent, harmful price discrimination should be absent.

Performance Criteria

   (i)   Production operations should be efficient.
  (ii)   Promotion costs should not be excessive.
 (iii)   Profits should be just sufficient to reward investment, efficiency and
       innovation.
 (iv)   Output levels and quality range should be responsive to consumer
       demand.
  (v)   Technological opportunities should be exploited, not suppressed.
 (vi)   Price setting behaviour should not intensify any general cyclical
       instability.
(vii)   Success should accrue to those who best satisfy consumer wants.

Source: Derived from S.H. Sosnick, 'A critique of concepts of workable
          competition', Quarterly Journal of Economics 1958.

unable to predict the presence and purpose of profits. Profits, according to the concentration doctrine, should *not* exist in an optimal equilibrium situation; they will exist in a concentrated market. The paucity of support for this theory is due to its inability to embrace the true role of profits and prices.

In a catallaxy, however, in a spontaneous order produced by a market, social welfare objectives cannot be defined in advance. Prices differing from marginal costs, differing marginal evaluations, the opportunity to grasp profit, must exist, *ab initio,* if two persons are to engage in mutually beneficial trading exchange. And secondly, the incentive of profits is required to motivate potential entrepreneurs (be they producers, consumers, resource-owners or 'pure' entrepreneurial middlemen) to be alert to the possibility of as yet unperceived opportunities. The taking in the future of unknown and unknowable chance precludes the laying down in the present of any social welfare function such as 'equality', 'social justice', 'Pareto optimality' or whatever. A catallaxy cannot be judged by its success in achieving such (indefinable) objectives. Rather an industrial organisation or structure must be assessed by its ability to provide the motivation (i.e. profits) to alert existing or potential entrepreneurs to improving the extent to which consumer tastes are satisfied.

(d) PUBLIC POLICY IMPLICATIONS

Viewed from an instant in time, profits may appear to be 'monopolistic', resulting from 'output restriction'. Profits, however, should be analysed by anti-trust legislators and others over the long run. Provided they arose from an entrepreneurial act which had as its aim the making of these profits then they should be approved of, not condemned. Any policy which minimises the fruits of entrepreneurial endeavour can only reduce such endeavour in the future. Even in the case where the entrepreneur has gained monopolistic control of a resource (and even if that resource was acquired with a view to reaping profits in the future from a sole ownership position), provided only that no other producers had yet perceived the importance consumers would attach to the product, then at the time of acquisition of sole control of the resource every part of the entrepreneur's plan meant an improvement in resource allocation, as viewed by consumers, over alternative entrepreneurial plans.*

---

* Only if other producers *had* perceived the value consumers would place on the employment of the resource in the particular use, but had merely failed to perceive the *additional* profits which would accrue from sole control, would this cease to be true. Then, in the absence of the entrepreneurial act, the resource would have been more or less rapidly exploited in line with consumer wishes. The normative implications are then ambiguous.

Policy makers should also avoid making conjectures or statements about which form of industrial organisation is the most 'efficient' or about the 'wastes' of product differentiation, duplication or advertising. Mergers have been encouraged or prevented over the years by governments in most industrial countries. Asset divestiture or merger prevention is the other side of the same coin. Yet the implication of catallactics is that no one has sufficient omniscience to judge which form of market structure is the most efficient for the meeting of tomorrow's consumer needs. The profit motivated entrepreneur is certainly not omniscient. But he will in most cases have a greater understanding than a bureaucrat of any present and possible future market conditions in the market area in which he is particularly interested. He will certainly have a greater motivation than the bureaucrat (entrepreneurial profit) to meet anticipated consumer demand.

Unless there are impediments to entrepreneurship (barriers to the exploitation of profitable opportunities) industries will mutate and evolve according to the principle of the division of labour and as guided by the invisible hand. This will not result in inefficient industrial organisation since the 'best' decisions will be taken at any given time, given the availability of knowledge at that time. When governments positively encourage a different form of industrial structure to emerge from that which would result autonomously, then the presumption must be that *that* form of organisation is inefficient (in the sense that a superior course of action that might have been taken has been avoided). Government-structured industry will be the result of less-well informed decisions, and of decisions motivated by factors other than the satisfying of consumer tastes and the making of profit.*

---

* Anticipated consumer demand is not the same thing as anticipated *voter* desires. Even if all citizens as consumers stand to gain from a *laissez-faire* policy, *particular* citizens as employees or investors stand to gain from *particular* interventions. The gains to particular pressure groups are always more overt, although less than, the diffuse gains to all consumers. Government thus finds it easier to accede to the desires of well-organised pressure groups than to consumer demand.

Similarly, the various aspects of product differentiation should not be condemned — even if *ex post* they appear to have been duplicative and wasteful. No one condemns, *ex post,* an engineer who in 1900 employed the best practice techniques of that year, albeit they were not the best practice techniques of 1980. The engineer of 1900 did not know — in that year — what techniques would be available in 1980. Similarly, in a catallaxy there is imperfect knowledge which the entrepreneur steadily improves — although this 'improvement' is towards an ever-receding goal. Thus each step in the competitive process, each decision to advertise, to duplicate, to price shade, to product differentiate, is a step towards improving coordination, towards equating marginal valuations of buyers and sellers. *No perceived opportunity* for improving resource allocation is left ungrasped (the 1900 situation). The fact that this involves what traditional welfare economists call competitive 'waste' is irrelevant (judging 1900 from the 1980 situation). The corollary of this is that if government attempts to intervene in the competitive process today by curbing advertising, product related services, product differentiation or whatever, *it is deliberately rejecting* opportunities to improve resource allocation as perceived by those most strongly motivated to search out and exploit them (entrepreneurs).

Finally, what implications does catallactics have for public utility regulation or for control of nationalised industries? What are the incentives for a nationalised or publicly regulated industry to act entrepreneurially, to seek out what the consumer wants and provide it? The answer is none. The actions of the managers of nationalised industries can be analysed from the theory of marginal cost pricing as in Chapter 3, section (d). There it was shown that even adherence to the rules of marginal cost pricing can result in substantial organisational slack (or X-inefficiency as some term it). Or the theory of bureaux discussed in Chapter 7, section (d) can be applied. The industries are run to provide benefits for certain powerful pressure groups, particularly employees/managers, some suppliers and some customers. 'In an important sense, nationalisation is not intended to secure the efficient allocation of resources, but to *prevent* it.'[7] (Emphasis in original.) Given that politicians, public utility managers and civil servants, are all human beings and given that each, like every human being, wishes to maximise his personal satisfaction, this is not surprising. A bureaucrat who adopts a conservative policy in administering or directing a nationalised industry stands little risk of personal loss in salary, status or prestige. He may even have a high probability of personal gain if his policies favour readily identifiable beneficiaries (such as those employees living in a particular politician's parliamentary constituency). On the other hand, a bureaucrat who adopts a non-conservative policy because he perceives consumers at large might benefit and so resources be allocated more efficiently stands (a) a high probability of personal loss if his perceptions are wrong; (b) a high probability of personal loss if his perceptions are correct but vocal and powerful pressure groups can express their disapproval before the benefits of his correct perceptions are reaped by consumers at large; and (c) a low probability of personal gain if his perceptions are correct but (as is usual in nationalised industries) his remuneration is linked in no way to his performance.

In short, the opportunity costs of any government policy towards industry are difficult to quantify, since by definition they are forgone benefits which never materialise. This is the challenge of industrial organisation as a subject. It is also the challenge *to* industrial organisation. It must cease to be seen as 'a field in deep intellectual trouble'. It has definite policy implications to offer. The suggested policies are diametrically opposed to those of the *dirigiste.* Yet justifying the claim that government intervention is harmful is both difficult and unfashionable.

To appreciate the costs of public policy 'requires imagination and understanding'.[7] Professor Littlechild spells out the role of the industrial economist. It is 'to trace out the implications . . . which others may not wish to do, or may not be able to do . . . (but) analysis by academics can stimulate entrepreneurship on the part of voters. It can make them aware of hitherto unappreciated merits or demerits of familiar policies and it can introduce them to new policies.' Just as advertising can encourage the consumer to be his own entrepreneur and to seek out and choose ways of improving his private consumption position, so industrial organisation, as a discipline, may help the voter to improve his public consumption position by seeking out for tomorrow those politicians and those policies which today would be deemed 'politically unacceptable'.

REFERENCES

1 G.L.S. Shackle, *Epistemics and Economics*, Cambridge 1972, p. 76.
2 L. von Mises, *Human Action* (3rd edition), Regnery 1966, pp. 122, 332.
3 J.M. Clark, 'Towards a concept of workable competition', *American Economic Review* 1940.
4 J.M. Clark, *Competition as a Dynamic Process*, Brookings Institution 1961, p. 490.
5 Clark (1961), p. ix.
6 Sir John Hicks, 'Some questions of time in economics', in A.M. Tung, F.M. Westfield and J.S. Worley (eds), *Evolution, Welfare and Time in Economics: Essays in Honour of Nicholas Georgescu-Ruegen*, Lexington 1976.
7 S.C. Littlechild, *Change Rules, O.K.?*, Inaugural Lecture, Birmingham University 1977, p. 15.

Index